BIBLICAL DAN

AVRAHAM BIRAN

BIBLICAL DAN

ISRAEL EXPLORATION SOCIETY

HEBREW UNION COLLEGE — JEWISH INSTITUTE OF RELIGION

JERUSALEM 1994

BIBLICAL DAN

ISBN 965–221–020–X

© 1994 the Israel Exploration Society

This book is an edited, revised and augmented
translation from the Hebrew, of the author's
Dan: 25 Years of Excavation of Tel Dan, Tel Aviv:
Hakibbutz Hameuchad and Israel Exploration Society, 1992.

English version: Joseph Shadur
Administrative editor: Joseph Aviram
Typeset and printed in Israel by Keterpress Enterprises, Jerusalem

CONTENTS

PREFACE

When early in 1966 three members of Kibbutz Dan in the north of Israel came to report that the antiquities at Tel Dan were being threatened, I could not foresee that 27 years later we would still be engaged in unravelling the mysteries of two ancient cities — Laish and Dan. I was at the time Director of the Department of Antiquities and Museums of the Ministry of Education and Culture, and the three who came to see me — Meir Rogni, David Amir and Elimelech Horowitz — were members of a unique volunteer organization, Trustees of Antiquities, dedicated to keeping watch over the country's historical heritage. They reported that the Israel Defense Forces were digging trenches and building gun emplacements on Tel Dan, endangering the ancient remains beneath the surface. Our Trustees urged us to initiate a rescue operation before it was too late.

Hastening to the site, we saw that they were right. The Syrian army was building up across the nearby border and the Israel military were fortifying Tel Dan and turning it into a major stronghold. Clearly, a rescue excavation was called for. We had to learn as much as possible before the ravages of war would make archaeological investigation difficult or even impossible.

The members of Kibbutz Dan were interested in the archaeological excavation for yet another reason. Their settlement is named after biblical Dan, and they sought archaeological evidence to confirm the identification of the mound next to their kibbutz. Moreover, the trees being planted on the site as camouflage and for additional security would hamper future excavations. I concluded that an expedition must be organized immediately.

When we began exploring the site in order to decide where to begin our rescue excavation we were not primarily concerned with its identification. As it happened, the decision where to sink our spade was actually made for us. The military authorities insisted that we excavate in a protected area, beyond the sights of the Syrian gunners. We thus had no choice but to begin our excavation on the southern slopes of the mound. This determined our excavation strategy in the years to come.

The first expedition of the Department of Antiquities and Museums comprised staff of the Department and workers from Qiryat Shemona provided by the Ministry of Labor employment service. In subsequent years our workers came mainly from the villages of Raja and ʿEin Qinyah. Following my retirement from the Department in 1974, I was appointed Director of the Nelson Glueck School of Biblical Archaeology of the Hebrew Union College-Jewish Institute of Religion, and the excavations at Tel Dan then became the project of the School and one of the major archaeological excavations in the country. A joint expedition was formed comprising the Nelson Glueck School of Biblical Archaeology, the Department of Antiquities and Museums and the Harvard Semitic Museum. The project now took on a cosmopolitan character with the core staff, supervisors, students and volunteers, primarily from the United States, Europe and Israel.

It is a truism that the success of an archaeological expedition is the result of team work and especially of its staff. In the course of 27 years there have been many changes in the composition of the staff. Some worked for many seasons, others for only one or two. To all of them I am indebted. In mentioning them I am well aware that merely naming them does not do them justice. I know that many have continued their archaeological research in other institutions and other expeditions, and have contributed greatly to the advancement and progress of archaeological research in Israel and abroad.

In listing the staff members of the Tel Dan expedition from 1966 to 1993 I am aware that some would be inadvertently omitted, and to them I offer my apologies and beg their indulgence: D. Amir (1966–1968, 1971–1972, 1976), E. Arieli (1968), W. Aufrecht (1982–1985), D. Bahat (1966–1969), R. Bar Nathan (1977–1979), P. Baublitz (1974–1975), D. Bechar (1979), R. Ben Dov (1982–1993), R. Blaushield (1971–1972), R. Bonfil (1986), O. Borowski (1974), R. Bullard (1974), D. Chuli (1982), N. Cohen (1978–1989), G. Cook (1975–1993), Y. Danieli (1985), G. Edelstein (1966–1969), M. Feist (1969–1974), F. Frick (1978), Z. Gal (1988), R. Goren (1974–1992), S. Goudowitz (1967), R. Hallote (1991), N. Heidebrecht (1984–1985), M. Hershkovitz (1981–1993), O. Hess (1972–1974), R. Hestrin (1975–1979), A. Higgs (1977–1980), H. Hirsch (1974–1991), T. Hirsch (1970–1971), D. Ilan (1988, 1991–1993), M. Kaplan (1974), K.A. Karein (1968–1970), E. Kessin (1977–1978), T. Levy (1988–1989, 1991), Y. Levy (1974), G. Mazor (1977–1981), G. Merker (1974–1975), H. Miller (1985), S. Millstein (1976), Y. Minsker (1971–1974), K.A. Moore (1974), S. Moshkowitz (1966–1969), Y. Nadelman (1982–1987), M.A.G. Nassar (1968–1970), A. Ogilvy (1972, 1974–1975), D. Packman (1975–1988), S. Paley (1970), R. Peled (1969, 1971), H. Pomerantz (1974), Y. Porat (1970–1975), R. Rohrbaugh

(1986), C. Scheepers (1988), K. Schoville (1979, 1981), E. Scoggin (1981–1982), B. Shantur (1970), M. Sharabani (1972), Y. Shoham (1981–1982, 1984, 1986), G. Solar (1976–1978, 1984–1986), C. Spencer (1982–1985, 1988), V. Tzaferis (1968–1978), R. Voss (1979–1987), S. Yaakobi (1969–1971), Z. Yeivin (1966–1969), S. Yisraeli (1966).

The financial cost of an archaeological expedition is enormous. Without the assistance of friends, foundations and institutions we could not have carried out our work these 27 years. They provided the means which enabled us to uncover a historical panorama extending from the Pottery Neolithic period of the 5th millennium B.C.E. to the 4th century of our era. I am grateful to all our friends who seek knowledge and insist on academic excellence. It would be a herculean task to mention them all and most of them would not want us to. And so in honoring them anonymously, I follow an ancient tradition. In the 6th-century C.E. synagogue at Jericho there is an Aramaic inscription near the entrance that reads (as translated by Prof. J. Naveh):

> Remembered for good be the memory of the
> entire holy community, the old and the
> young, whom the Lord of the universe
> aided, and were of strength, and made
> the mosaic. He who knows their names
> and those of their children and their
> families, may He inscribe them in the
> Book of Life, with all the pious, friends
> to all Israel. Peace, Amen

Having thus entrusted the names of our benefactors to immortality, I am duty bound to mention and give due credit to the Department of Antiquities and Museums of the Government of Israel, under whose auspices the excavations were begun, and to the Hebrew Union College-Jewish Institute of Religion, which since 1974 provided the means, staff, direction and encouragement to make Tel Dan one of the major archaeological undertakings in Israel. I am particularly indebted to the President of the Hebrew Union College-Jewish Institute of Religion, Dr. Alfred Gottschalk, for his continued interest, support and inspiration which enabled us to complete the task begun in 1966 and to present the results of our work in this volume.

Twenty-seven years of work at Tel Dan have shed much light on the history of this unique site, but our discoveries are far from telling the whole story. Out of the 200 dunams (50 acres) occupied by the site, only a little over 10 dunams (2½ acres) have been excavated until now — and of these we only reached bedrock in one small spot of 4 x 3 m. Nevertheless, from what has been cleared we have learned to expect many more discoveries. And indeed, as this book was being readied for printing a sensational find was made. At the edge of a stone-paved piazza, near a newly-discovered Israelite city-gate, a fragment of an inscribed stele came to light. The broken basalt slab bears thirteen truncated lines of Aramaic text which mentions a "king of Israel" and a "king of the House of David!" — the first mention of the royal name "David" ever found outside the Bible. Because of the great importance of this rare find, we decided, at the last moment, to add a postscript chapter describing the inscription.

This conveys something of the excitement of digging at Tel Dan. The archaeological finds of the past 27 years were published as they were being uncovered, and today the staff of the expedition labors at the preparation of the full and detailed report of the Tel Dan excavations from their beginning.

On the basis of this research, and with the help of the present members — R. Ben Dov, N. Cohen, G. Cook, M. Hershkowitz, H. Hirsch, D. Ilan, D. Packman — of the Nelson Glueck School of Biblical Archaeology of the Hebrew Union College-Jewish Institute of Religion, we are pleased to relate here the story of ancient Laish-Dan, chapter by chapter — not according to the chronological order of its discovery, but mainly in its historical sequence throughout the ages.

A. Biran
Jerusalem, 1994

STRATA AND CHRONOLOGY OF TEL DAN

Stratum	Archaeological Period	Date B.C.E.
XVI	Pottery Neolithic	5th millennium
XV	Early Bronze II	30th–
XIV	Early Bronze III	–23rd centuries
XIII	Middle Bronze I	23rd–20th centuries
XII	Middle Bronze IIA	20th–19th centuries
XI	Middle Bronze IIA–B	18th century
X	Middle Bronze IIB	18th–17th centuries
IX	Middle Bronze IIC	17th–16th centuries
VIII	Late Bronze I	16th–15th centuries
VII	Late Bronze II	14th–13th centuries
VI	Iron I	12th century
V	Iron I	12th–first half of 11th centuries
IVB	Iron I and II	second half of 11th– first half of 10th centuries
IVA	Iron II	second half of 10th–beginning 9th centuries
III	Iron II	9th–beginning 8th centuries
II	Iron II	second and third quarters of the 8th century
I	Iron II	end of 8th–early 6th centuries
	Persian	6th–4th centuries
	Hellenistic	4th–1st centuries
	Roman	1st century B.C.E.–4th C.E.

Illustrations

Note: All measurements and dimensions are metric — in centimeters for objects; in meters for architectural elements. In sections, all vertical heights are above seal-level.

Color Plates

37. Faience die
38. Figurine of the god Bes
39. Bronze figurine of Osiris
40. Head of female figurine
41. Oil-lamp of the Roman period
42. Decorated amphoriskos
43. Two pithoi of the 7th century B.C.E. from Area T *in situ*
44. Base of the canopied structure

Staff members of the Tel Dan expedition meet to analyze and discuss the results of the day's field work

1. Tel Dan: view from the south at the beginning of the excavation

INTRODUCTION

"Why excavate?" is a question often heard. What is it that makes scholars and laymen undertake the sometimes hazardous task of excavating ancient remains. The classical answer given by Sir Edmund P. Hillary when asked why he climbed Mount Everest may be enough — "because it is there." Indeed, in many parts of the world, and especially in Israel, the countryside is dotted with sites and monuments begging for the hand and spade of the archaeologist. The insatiable intellectual curiosity and the search for knowledge are prime movers in the advancement of science in general and archaeological research in particular.

For those of us who were brought up on the Bible there is an urge to visualize, to touch, to reconstruct the past and its material culture. This compulsion extends to the remote past — to prehistoric times as well as to historic periods. If in reconstructing history and societies of prehistory we must rely solely on the material remains found in the course of excavations, for the later stages of human development we also have the invaluable resource of written evidence.

Tel Dan — Tell el-Qadi in Arabic, meaning Mound of the Judge — is situated at the foot of Mount Hermon on one of the three main sources of the Jordan River. The mound, which occupies 200 dunams (50 acres), was identified with the biblical city of Dan in 1838 by the American scholar-explorer Edward Robinson. It is the Dan at the northern limit of the country from the expression "From Dan to Beersheba," meaning the entire Land of Israel. As a place name Dan first appears in Genesis 14:14: "And when Abram heard that his brother was taken captive, he armed his trained servants...and pursued them unto Dan." However, we know that in the days of Abraham the name of the city was Laish. Judges 18:29 records: "And they called the name of the city Dan...howbeit the name of the city was Laish at the first." In Joshua 19:47 it is called Leshem.

The name Laish also appears in the Egyptian Execration Texts, in the Mari documents and in the records of Thutmose III of the mid–15th century B.C.E. Except for the name of its king Horon-ab mentioned in the 18th century B.C.E. Execration Texts, and information to the effect that tin was imported to Laish, the written sources tell us virtually nothing about the city at that time. Only from the five Danite spies who came to

2. Aerial view of Tel Dan (ca. 1940) without the trees that cover most of the mound
    today

Laish do we hear that the people there were "quiet and secure...far from the Zidonians, and had no business with any man." (Judges 18:7).

From the time that the tribe of Dan settled at the site the information we have, if still fragmentary, enables us to learn a little more of the city. Thus we are told that the "...children of Dan set up for themselves the graven image and Jonathan...and his sons were priests to the tribe of Dan..." (Judges 18:30).

Dan is mentioned in the census ordered by King David (1 Chronicles 21:2). The census-takers came to Dan from Gilead (2 Samuel 24:6). After the death of Solomon, Dan became a cult center in the 10th century B.C.E. King Jeroboam I of Israel set up a Golden Calf there, as related in 1 Kings 12:29. The city was attacked by Ben-hadad of Damascus at the beginning of the 9th century B.C.E., and in the 8th century B.C.E. the prophet Amos castigated the people of Israel for swearing by the "God of Dan." It is not mentioned as one of the cities conquered by the Assyrians but is referred to as the northern outpost of the country by the prophet Jeremiah (Jeremiah 4:15; 8:16). Finally, Dan appears in the lists of Eusebius in the 4th century C.E.

Today Tel Dan rises 18 m. above the surrounding plain. That the hill is an artificial, man-made mound was known a long time ago. The intrepid Scottish traveler, John MacGregor, who sailed his kayak from the sources of the Jordan to the Dead Sea in 1869, wrote that although the mound is said to be a volcanic crater, he himself had no doubt that it was artificial. And indeed, the slightly concave surface at the top of the mound has the appearance of an extinct volcano, and this impression is enhanced by the black basalt boulders there. MacGregor correctly described the artificial hill as "a mound of great size...its shape...rectangular, with rounded corners." MacGregor could not have known that the sides of the rectangle "like those of a railway viaduct" are in effect the upper part of a sloping earth rampart. The true significance of these slopes became clear to us already in the first season of excavation in 1966, when we had just begun the rescue dig.

A rescue excavation has certain limitations. From the beginning we wondered whether our archaeological explorations would support the identification of the site with ancient Laish and Dan, and if any evidence for the conquest of Laish or for the establishment of the sanctuary would come to light. However, fearing for our safety, the military authorities did not allow us to work at the northwestern part of the mound near the spring and restricted us to excavating at the southern side of the mound. We decided therefore to devote our efforts initially to investigating the nature and composition of the outer and inner slopes which gave the mound its distinctive topographic appearance.

From the top of the mound we opened a 2.5 m.-wide trench down the outer slope to ground level. We soon found that the slope was man-made and was composed of plaster-covered layers of earth. The main component of this plaster was travertine limestone deposited by the Dan Spring. The construction of the inner slope is similar, but in the middle — between the two opposing slopes — we discovered a monumental stone structure, about 6.5 m. wide, that served as the core for the huge embankment. The discovery of the circular ramparts with steep inward and outward slopes confirmed the views of scholars such as Benjamin Mazar and William F. Albright that Dan is to be included among the earliest cities of the ancient Middle East sheltering behind earthen ramparts. Some scholars hold that

3. Start of the excavation in 1966 between large protruding boulders at the southern
    flank of the mound; the trench is blocked by the core of the embankment

the erection of such massive earthen embankments of soil gathered from
the remains of earlier occupational strata and from virgin land of the adja-
cent plain was a defensive response to a new form of attack — the battering
ram. But earthen defensive ramparts have been found also at earlier sites
and until now it is impossible to determine where and when they appear
for the first time. It is certain however, that a considerable number of such
ramparts were built already in the 18th century B.C.E. The ramparts of
Tel Dan constitute one of the best examples.

Our trial trench was dug down the outer slope of the tell between large
boulders that protruded from the slope. The embankment formed the
immense defensive system of the ancient city of Laish, the precursor of
Dan. These ramparts appeared to be similar to those uncovered at many
sites in the ancient East that were built during the 2nd millennium B.C.E.
The intriguing problem of the ramparts and their construction became a
subject of major interest to us in the course of subsequent seasons, also when
we were no longer confined to the southern sector. Thirteen years later
we discovered the unique triple arched gate of the 18th century B.C.E.,
one of the most important architectural discoveries in the entire Near East.

Following the Six-Day War we were able to extend our excavations to all parts of the large mound and to open a number of excavation grid squares in the northern section of the site to penetrate deeply into the tell, near the fresh-water spring. It is here that the remains of the sanctuary precinct were eventually uncovered — probably the place where Jeroboam I set up the Golden Calf. It was in this area that any doubts we may have had about the identification of the site were finally laid to rest: A dedicatory bilingual inscription of the Hellenistic period, in ancient Greek and Aramaic, mentioning the "God who is in Dan" confirmed what had first been suggested a century-and-a-half ago by Edward Robinson.

Still, the unknown far outweighs the discoveries to date. The panorama set out in the following pages can only foreshadow what the future holds in store.

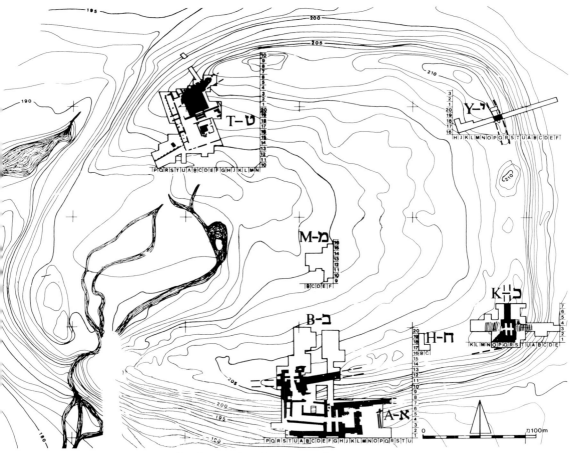

4. Topographic map of Tel Dan showing excavation areas

CHAPTER I — THE NEOLITHIC PERIOD

In the beginning there was only water. The wide expanse of the Tethys Sea covered all of today's Galilee and the Golan Heights. There came a time when the sea receded and a land of mountains, plains and valleys was formed. One such valley, the Jordan Valley, was part of the Great Rift extending from Asia Minor to Central Africa. Eons of geological upheavals and volcanic eruptions left snow-capped Mount Hermon looming high into the clouds. The lake that touched the slopes of the mountain began to recede southward, and a large alluvial plain of fertile soil remained. The melting snows of Mount Hermon and the abundant rainfall fed the perennial springs of Dan whose gushing waters become the river Dan — one of the three tributaries of the Jordan. These waters irrigate the fertile soil of the plain while the slopes of Mount Hermon provide good grazing land and easy passage for travelers plying the trade routes between the major centers of ancient civilization in Mesopotamia, the Mediterranean shores and Egypt.

The low hill, somewhat higher than the surrounding plain, was ideal for human habitation. Indeed, from the beginning we were sure that because of its situation and fertile surroundings a settlement must have existed at our site long before the one of the 3rd millennium B.C.E. that we were uncovering. But only after 17 seasons of excavations, in 1984, in a deep narrow trench of Area B in the southern section of the excavation, at an incredible depth of 13 m. (almost 40 feet) beneath the surface, part of a wall built of large fieldstones and a floor abutting it were uncovered about 50 cm. above bedrock. The wall is 80 cm. wide and has been preserved to a height of two to three courses. The sherds found on and in the floor are of the Pottery-Neolithic period at the beginning of the 5th millennium B.C.E. — our Stratum XVI. Despite the small area under excavation the evidence was enough to show that these early inhabitants of Tel Dan already had a fairly well developed material culture.

At that period pottery vessels made their first appearance. Although the ceramic find in Stratum XVI was meager, it nevertheless represents the overall achievements in the field of pottery — the beginning of a rich ceramic tradition in the Land of Israel. The clay contained both sand-grit and gravel, as well as straw to give the material flexibility and strength in

firing and cooking. Vessels made to hold liquids were covered with a slip
to render them watertight. Among the finds are a basalt pedestal bowl, storage jars, bowls, amphoriskoi and flint tools which include sickle blades,
arrowheads, axes, burins, a scraper and bone tools. Under a floor was a burial of an infant interred in a jar. To allow the insertion of the six-month
old infant, part of the jar was removed and the wall of a second jar was
used as a cover for the burial. Another jar was found accompanied by many
sherds of a vessel similar to that which covered the burial jar. Possibly it
served a similar purpose, though no skeletal remains were found. Of 144
animal bones recovered in the small probe, 69 could be identified. The species represented were domestic cattle, goat and sheep, pig (probably wild
boar) an equid (probably a donkey), and a dog.

How extensive the Pottery-Neolithic settlement of Tel Dan was and
what activities these early inhabitants engaged in we can only surmise. The
accumulation of 2 m. of debris of this period, representing five sub-phases

5.   Pottery-Neolithic period wall (Stratum XVI) below an Early Bronze Age pebble
     floor

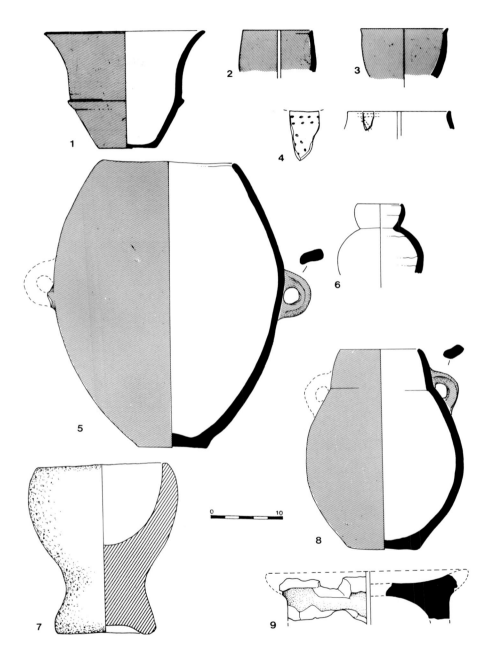

6. Finds of the Pottery-Neolithic period (Stratum XVI): 1–4 — bowls;
   5 — hole-mouth jar; 6, 8 — amphoriskoi; 7 — basalt chalice (see Fig. 7);
   9 — pottery stand

of occupation, points to the considerable size of the Late Neolithic settlement at Dan, which lasted perhaps a few hundred years. When in the 1989 season, in Area T at the northern end of the site, we uncovered part of another wall of the same period, the existence of a large community in the 5th millennium B.C.E. was confirmed. Some remains of this period were also discovered in a small probe in Area M, at the center of the site.

We do not know what happened to these early inhabitants. They seemed to have disappeared, or perhaps they were killed off. The evidence we have shows the site to have been largely unoccupied for nearly a thousand years. The next chapter in the history of Tel Dan begins in the 3rd millennium B.C.E., in the Early Bronze II period when a large settlement was established at the site.

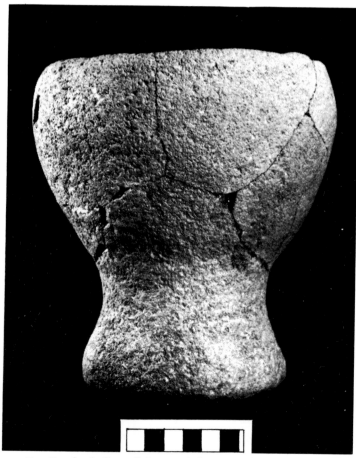

7. Basalt chalice of the Neolithic period (see Fig. 6:7)

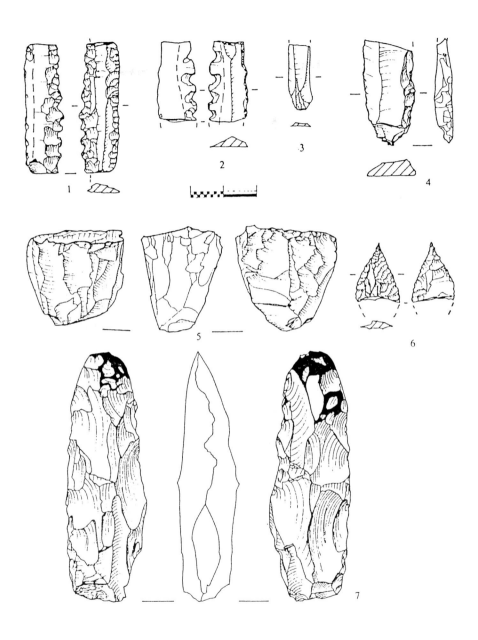

8. Flint tools of the Pottery-Neolithic period (Stratum XVI): 1,2 — sickle blades;
    3 — small obsidian blade; 4 — chipped blade; 5 — flint core; 6 — arrowhead;
    7 — axe

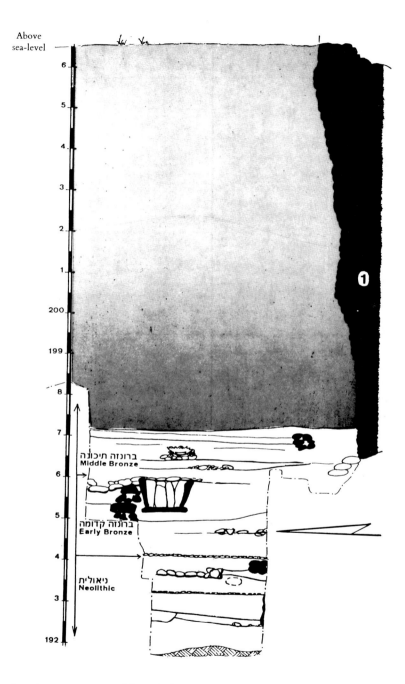

9.   Section showing stone core (1) and the earlier levels of settlement under the
     rampart embankment.

CHAPTER II — THE FIRST URBAN SETTLEMENT IN THE EARLY BRONZE AGE

Already during the first season of excavations in 1966 we were impressed by the huge quantity of Early Bronze Age sherds which seemed to indicate the existence of an extensive settlement here in the 3rd millennium B.C.E. This assumption was confirmed in the course of subsequent excavation seasons: Early Bronze Age sherds were found in practically every basket of excavated material.

In the 3rd millennium B.C.E. — the Early Bronze Age — occurred the urban development in the region extending from the Euphrates to the Nile Valley. The Bible tells of the days when people said to each other "Go to, let us build us a city..." (Genesis 11:3–4). In the land which is today Israel, as in the neighboring countries, many urban settlements were established for the first time. It was probably the development of irrigated agriculture that spurred the growth of urban life in the upper Jordan Valley. The hill by the springs of the Jordan River was especially conducive to permanent residence and to the development of an urban center. The city must have had a name. Perhaps it was the same name by which it was known in the 2nd millennium B.C.E. — Laish, meaning Lion, perhaps after the lions in the thickets along the banks of the Jordan. Jeremiah 49:19, the Song of Songs 4:8, and Deuteronomy 33:22 all attest to the presence of lions in the region. We have not yet found the remains of the Early Bronze Age fortifications, public buildings, palaces, temples and sanctuaries. Nevertheless, we feel justified in calling Laish a city because a settlement of such proportions would have required urban services and administration. No doubt, somewhere within the large area occupied by the Early Bronze Age settlement, such structures exist and will come to light in future excavations.

The Early Bronze Age city probably occupied an area of more than 200 dunams or 50 acres. An archaeological surface survey carried out by members of our expedition in the region showed the other ancient settlements to have been smaller. Using standard demographic criteria based on anthropological studies, the population of the city probably numbered four to five thousand. Our estimate of the size of the city was derived from undisturbed structural remains uncovered in various parts of the mound.

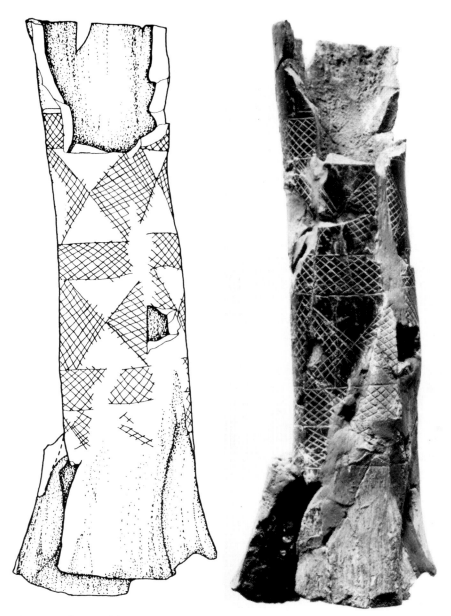

10.   Decorated animal bone (sword handle) of the Early Bronze Age

During the first seasons of excavations in Area A, beneath the layers of the outer slope of the rampart material, the floor of a building and remnants of a wall were found. On the floor rested a storage jar and a badly burnt decorated bone cylinder 19.5 cm. long and about 6 cm. in diameter —

11. Early Bronze Age storage jar *in situ* (see Fig. 12)

apparently the hilt of a sword. The jar, a large, combed metallic ware pithos, was damaged in antiquity by the construction of a tomb in a later period. Fear of collapse in the narrow, 2.5 m.-wide, but extremely deep trench excavated at the foot of the rampart forced us to abandon further excavation in this 5 sq. m. area. However, nine years later, in Area Y, along the northeastern flank of the mound, more Early Bronze Age remains were uncovered.

In this excavation area, we reached the Early Bronze Age strata in the course of our investigation of the sloping stone core construction, beneath the layers of earth of the inner Middle Bronze Age ramparts. Here again, only a small area of about 2 sq. m. was excavated. Three phases of occupation could be discerned. A relatively large number of broken vessels was found — typical Early Bronze platters, jars, bowls and juglets. A complete comb-pattern jar discovered *in situ*, standing on a floor, is a fine and important example of the period's material culture. Remains of the Early Bronze period were also found near the base of the rampart, on its outer slope some 50 m. east of the standing jar.

12.   The storage jar after restoration (see Fig. 11)

Additional architectural remains of the Early Bronze Age were also
uncovered in 1982 in Area K after we removed a few of the stone steps
from the staircase leading from the eastern gate down to the street of the
2nd millennium B.C.E. city. About 30 cm. beneath the steps, we found
two stone walls at right angles to each other. The walls, preserved to a

height of 1 m., and the floor of large flagstones next to them may indicate that this was a building of some importance. About 80 cm. below the floor another wall was uncovered. The massive construction of these remains and their location suggested that perhaps here was the Early Bronze Age city gate. A little further west, at the end of the staircase, a bonded corner and two thick walls were found providing further tantalizing evidence of the Early Bronze Age city.

We were greatly tempted to uncover more of the Early Bronze Age buildings in Area K, but to do so would have required the removal of the monumental steps of the subsequent Middle Bronze Age — an equally important period of early urbanization. This sort of problem always puts the archaeologist in a quandary — how much of one level should be removed to reach earlier ones? In this case, for the time being, we decided to keep as many of the steps leading from the gate as possible, hoping to learn more of Early Bronze Laish from other excavation sites on the tell.

The clearest sequence of Early Bronze Age occupation came from the deep probe in Area B, where the stratified Neolithic remains had been reached. Here, the first Early Bronze Age settlement, dated to the 27th century B.C.E., is represented by an occupation surface at an elevation of 194.04 m. above sea level and by a cobblestone floor at 194.15 m. — about 12 m. below the present surface of the mound. Seven phases of occupation could be discerned belonging to the Early Bronze II (Stratum XV) and

13. Early Bronze Age II–III metallic-ware vessels

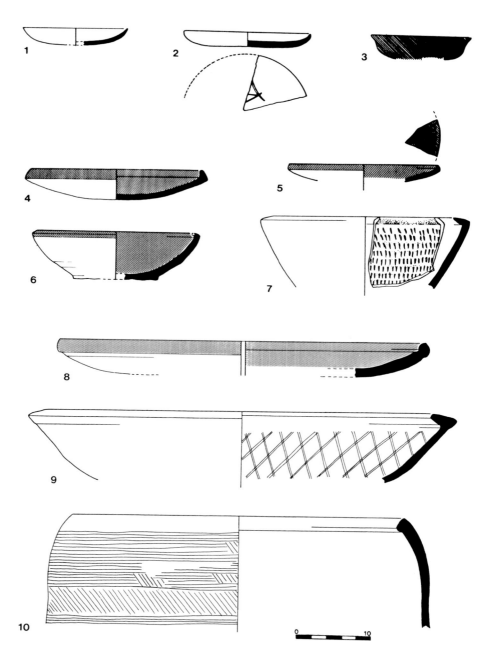

14.   Pottery vessels of the Early Bronze Age II–III (Stratum XIV–XV):
      1–3, 6, 7,9 — bowls; 4, 5, 8 — platters; 10 — krater

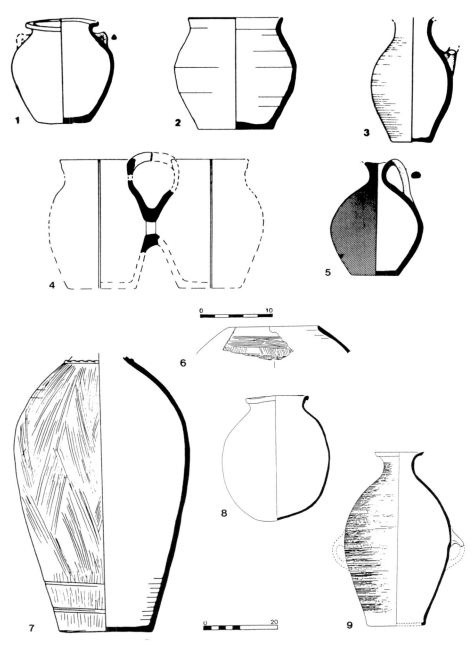

15. Pottery vessels of the Early Bronze Age II–III (Stratum XIV–XV):
     1, 2 — amphoriskoi; 3, 5 — jugs; 4 — double-jug; 6, 8 — cooking pots;
     7 — pithos; 9 — jar

Early Bronze III (Stratum XIV) periods, between the 27th and 24th centuries B.C.E. Remains of walls, floors, a silo and a destruction level characterize this period. Pottery vessels which include cooking pots, pithoi, jugs, large and small amphoras, bowls as well as a grind-stone — all found in the small area we excavated — are indicative of the rich material culture of the inhabitants. The various vessels are primarily household artifacts representing a continuous ceramic tradition.

The pottery of the Early Bronze Age was mostly made by hand, except for small vessels, mainly bowls that were thrown on a wheel. The potters of the period learned to sort and mix clay in order to adapt their pots to various uses. Cooking pots contain quartzite and calcite that impart flexibility and resistance to high temperatures. Amphoras were fired at high temperatures in order to seal the pores in the clay. A special category of vessels, known as "metallic" are typical of the late Early Bronze III period, mainly in northern Israel, Syria and Lebanon. Amphoras and jugs of this type were found in the tombs of kings and the aristocracy in Old Kingdom Egypt, and they attest to extensive commercial relations in that period. We were surprised not to find more of the beautiful, highly-polished Beth Yeraḥ (Khirbet Kerak) ware, which is found in abundance at other sites in the Jordan Valley and is so typical of the Early Bronze III period in northern Israel. Although a few scattered sherds were found in the other areas of the excavation, no conclusions can as yet be drawn as to their importance in the material culture of the inhabitants at that time.

We do not know the ethnic composition of the proto-historic inhabitants of Laish and for lack of a better term we shall refer to them as Canaanites. Of the life and customs of the people we know very little. From the animal bones examined we know that they possessed goats and sheep which provided them with wool, hair, milk and meat; cattle may have been used in plowing and threshing. They supplemented their diet by hunting fallow deer, some of whose bones bear cut marks that usually occur on domestic animals and which indicate that the animals were killed and consumed on the spot. The flint tools found include typical Early Bronze Age sickle blades and tabular scrapers made of good quality dark-brown flint. Only two copper objects of the Early Bronze Age were found at Laish — in the unstratified fill of the earthen ramparts — an axehead and an adze dated on typological grounds to the second half of the 3rd millennium B.C.E. These tools may point to trade relations.

It is difficult to ascertain the function of many of the small finds of the period uncovered in the course of the excavation. A button seal found in the earth fill of the ramparts is unique in this country. It is made of gray limestone with a geometric design on its flat face, and may have been an

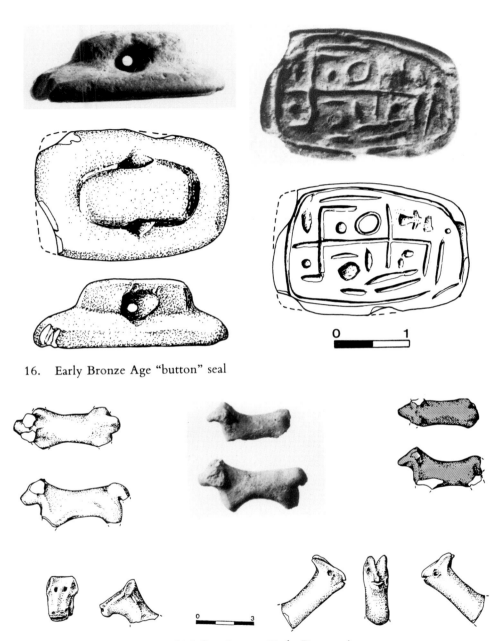

16. Early Bronze Age "button" seal

17. Clay animal (zoomorphic) figurines — Early Bronze Age

import either from the North (Syria or Mesopotamia) or from Egypt. The many fragments of pottery figurines of animals may have been just toys, or they may have served a symbolic or totemistic function, perhaps related

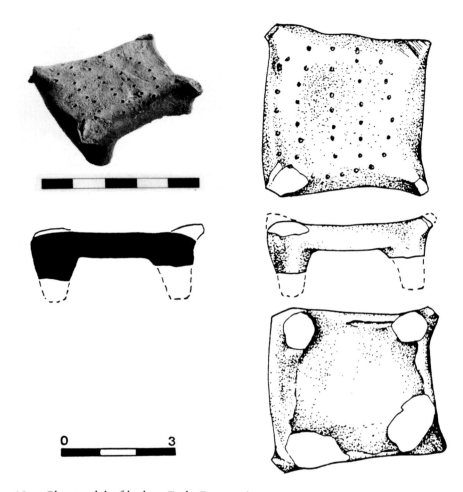

18.   Clay model of bed — Early Bronze Age

to a cult practice. The same might be said for the model couches or beds,
4.3 cm.-square, one of which was found nearly complete, with a foot at
each corner and a horn-like projection above, and the top surface decorated
with pin-pricks before firing. Only five such model beds have been found
in the country. These clay models are somewhat similar to Mesopotamian
examples which seem to be connected with fertility rites.

   An important repertoire of 22 cylinder seal impressions, similar to others
found elsewhere in the country, has come to light in our excavations —
the largest number found at any site in Israel. Some scholars have suggested
that they represent cultic practices of Early Bronze III and could mean that
Laish was a center of seal production. The seal impressions include herring-

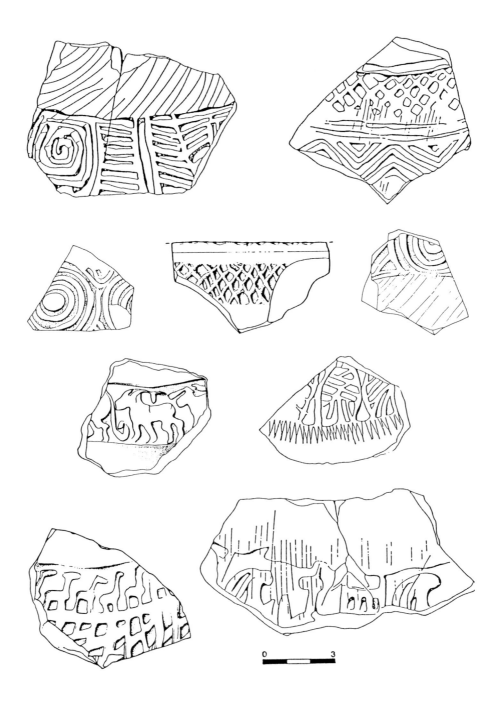

19. Cylinder seal impressions of the Early Bronze Age II–III

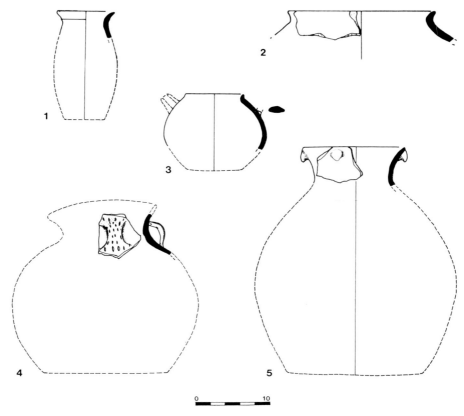

20. Middle Bronze Age I sherds (Stratum XIII) and the vessels they represent:
     1 — goblet; 2 — cooking pot; 3 — pot; 4 — amphoriskos; 5 — jar

bone designs, concentric circles or spirals, net and wavy lines, spiral and
linear motifs, and animals. Possibly one example may represent a human
figure, a part of a structure, and a horned animal. The arms of the figure
are extended upward, perhaps representing a man at prayer.

What brought an end to the Early Bronze Age civilization at Laish is
not clear. Established around 2700 B.C.E., the city grew and developed,
reached its zenith around 2500 B.C.E., and ceased around 2400 B.C.E.
There is no evidence of violent destruction, but the areas excavated are too
small to enable us to determine the nature of whatever calamity befell the
city. Many cities in the country were abandoned around the 24th century
B.C.E. Whether this was due to an act of nature such as climatic change,
or through human action such as degradation of the environment, will
have to await further research.

However, Laish was not completely deserted. In at least two of the excavation areas, remains were found which are attributed to a period sometimes called Middle Bronze I, Early Bronze IV, or Transitional Early Bronze-Middle Bronze, at the end of the 3rd millennium and the beginning of the 2nd millennium B.C.E. (Stratum XIII). The pottery vessels discovered are similar to those in the tombs of Middle Bronze I at Ma'ayan Barukh and Tel Kadesh, both a few kilometers west of Dan. It is quite possible that somewhere on Tel Dan more substantial evidence of settlement from this period will be turned up by the spade of the archaeologist.

CHAPTER III — THE SECOND URBAN REVOLUTION — THE MIDDLE BRONZE AGE IIA

The 2nd millennium B.C.E. dawned at Laish with no hint as to the momentous events that would shape the history of the city in the following centuries. It was during this period that the massive sloping ramparts were built, giving the mound the topography it has today. But this did not happen immediately, and over two hundred years passed before the inhabitants defended their city by erecting this monumental fortification.

The archaeological term for the first half of the 2nd millennium B.C.E. is the Middle Bronze II Period, with a number of subdivisions. For convenience's sake we follow the terminology and dates of the *New Encyclopedia*

21.   Upper part of a Middle Bronze Age IIA pithos

of Archaeological Excavations of the Holy Land, published by the Israel Exploration Society and the Massada Press, Jerusalem, 1993. Evidence for sedentary occupation of Laish during the beginning of the 2nd millennium
B.C.E. — the Middle Bronze IIA period — (Stratum XII) was discovered
early in our excavations. At the foot of the southern slope, in Area A, under
the mass of earth which comprises the earthen ramparts, an undisturbed
stone-built cist tomb was found beneath a floor of beaten earth. The tomb
could be only partially excavated because it is located at the bottom of a
narrow trench. A single bowl and a few sherds found next to the skull of
the deceased provided the Middle Bronze IIA dating of this tomb.

A sort of technological revolution in pottery manufacture occurred in
the Middle Bronze period: almost all the vessels were now thrown on a
fast wheel (except for a certain type of cooking pot with a flat base). At
the beginning of the period we see a great deal of variety in vessel form,
but toward the middle of the millennium the forms became standardized
as a result of mass-production — perhaps in pottery-making centers that
supplied a larger area. The potter's art reached a zenith at the time. Still
today it arouses wonderment at the technical proficiency, and modern potters try hard to imitate these ancient vessels. Usually, the most common
forms of the Middle Bronze period represent continuity from Early Bronze
period pottery. However, some of the forms recall types known from Syria
and Mesopotamia, such as large bowls and narrow-mouth cooking-pots,
and later, large, white bowls and brown-colored juglets. These vessels, as
well as the burial practices, apparently indicate contacts with Syria and
Mesopotamia, and perhaps also population movements from there.

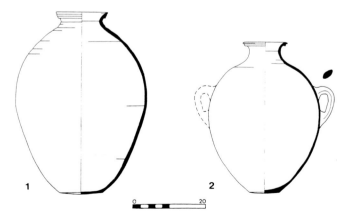

22.   Storage jars of the Middle Bronze Age IIA (Stratum XII)

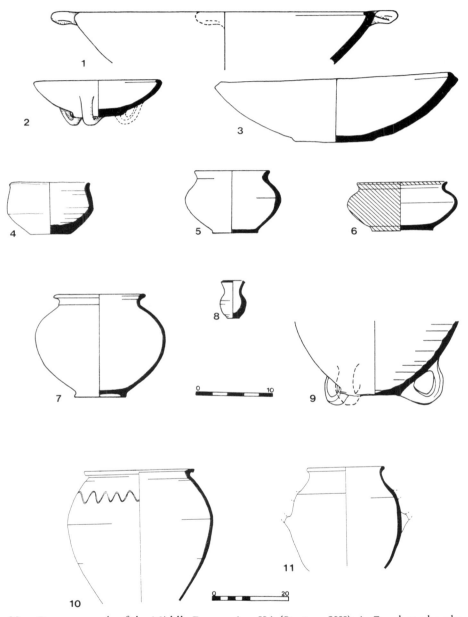

23. Pottery vessels of the Middle Bronze Age IIA (Stratum XII): 1–7 — large bowls; 8 — goblet; 9–11 — kraters

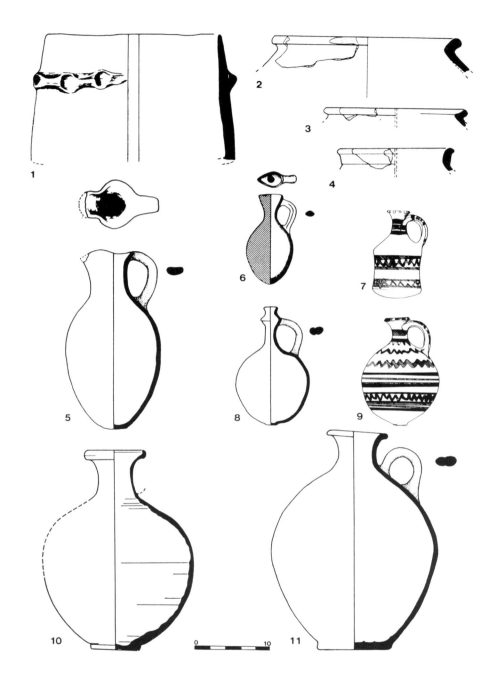

24.   Pottery vessels of the Middle Bronze Age IIA (Stratum XII): 1–4 — cooking
      pots; 6–9 — juglets; 5, 10, 11 — jugs

Further stratigraphic evidence of the Middle Bronze IIA settlement came to light when we attempted to reach bedrock in Area B. The exterior north face of the rampart's stone core was cleared in a very narrow section. Below the level of the stone core the opening of an excavation square revealed three, or possibly four, phases of Middle Bronze IIA occupation. Remains of a wall, floors and a well-built stone cist burial confirmed the existence of a permanent settlement at that time.

The tomb (No. 4244), measuring 85 x 64 cm. and 40 cm. high on the inside, was embedded under a plaster floor and constructed of large and medium-sized basalt fieldstones. The tomb was roofed with stone slabs and the floor was of beaten earth. Some of the stones used in constructing the cist tomb were taken from the latest Early Bronze levels encountered immediately beneath it. The tomb contained the skeleton of a child about six years of age, in a flexed position on its right side, in an east-west orientation with the head facing east. The only funerary offering was a juglet and some beads found next to the skull. The vessel is a lovely red-slipped and

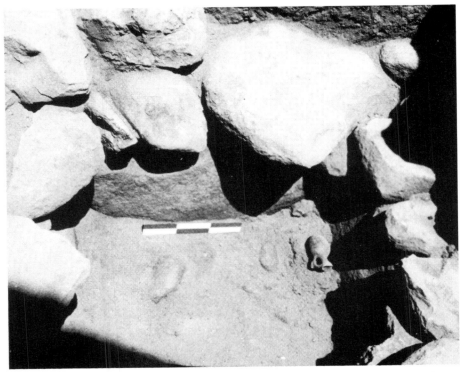

25.   Tomb 4244 with dipper juglet *in situ* — Middle Bronze Age IIA (see Fig. 26)

26.   The juglet from Tomb 4244 (Stratum XII) (see Figs. 25; 24:6)

burnished dipper juglet, classic for the Middle Bronze IIA period. The
beads are of semi-precious stones including amethyst, rock crystal and car-
nelian.

Additional information of the Middle Bronze IIA Age occupation was
obtained from the excavations in Area M at the center of the site, and from

Area Y at the northeast, but it is insufficient for completing the picture. We can only say that Laish of the 20–19th centuries B.C.E. was fairly large, perhaps as large as in the Early Bronze Age. We do not know who the people of the city were, and know very little about them. That the two tombs of the period excavated by us contained only one burial and one vessel each might mean that this was a less complex and less hierarchical society than the one after it.

The period between the Middle Bronze IIA and the Middle Bronze IIB may well deserve a special designation. Yet there is no consensus among scholars. For want of a better term we will call it the Transitional Middle Bronze IIA–B period which corresponds roughly to the 18th century B.C.E. (our Stratum XI). It may well have begun at the end of the 19th century B.C.E. It is an important period in the history of Laish, for it is during this time that the sloping earthen ramparts were built, giving the mound its present form.

A glimpse into the material culture of the people of the period is provided by Tomb 1025 discovered in Area Y, in the northeastern part of the city. The tomb is rectangular, constructed chiefly of basalt, although some limestone was also used. Its interior measurements are 2.15 x 1.35 m. by

27.   Tomb 1025: view from the interior showing the entrance with blocking stone

28.   Tomb 1025: view from the exterior after removal of the blocking stone

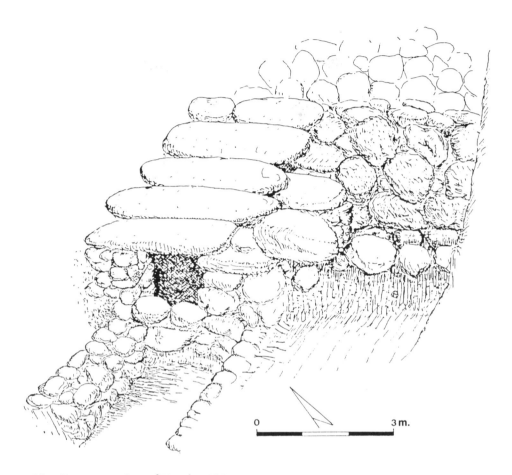

29. Reconstruction of Tomb 1025

90 cm. high. The walls of the tomb are erect. The basalt slab roof was laid over one course of smaller corbeled slabs which were set along the top of the longer north and south walls of the tomb. The exterior edges were weighted down by masses of stone and earth to counterbalance the corbeling. The entrance to the tomb is nearly square, 70 x 60 cm., and was found blocked by a single stone. Two east-west parallel walls flank the tomb entrance forming a dromos, or corridor, which could however, belong to an earlier period. The skeletal evidence consists of four individuals, all adults, the youngest being 19–20 years of age. The high moisture in the tomb precluded good preservation of human remains. No complete skeleton was found, but the undisturbed skeletal remains nearest the entry

30.   Bowls and juglets from Tomb 1025 (see drawings, Figs. 23 and 24)

showed some sign of articulation and may be assumed to comprise the latest burial. The remains of the other three interments had been pushed against the side of the tomb together with their accompanying offerings. These bones were fragmentary, and nothing even close to a complete skeleton was recovered. The poor state of preservation prevented us from determining such factors as orientation and position of interment, or the spatial relationships between burial goods and the bodies. The partially articulated skeletal remains found near the entrance indicate a contracted or semi-contracted position, in keeping with other burials of the period. The numerous funerary offerings, mainly pottery vessels, included 5 platters, 10 small globular bowls, 5 jugs, 9 juglets, a small carinated bowl, one krater and one lamp. Of special interest was a bronze dagger and pommel. The bones of a fallow deer and two goats or sheep were also part of the offering assemblage.

The limited data only allow us to say that the people (perhaps the family of the persons buried in our tomb) invested great effort and economic resources in ensuring a proper burial. The origin of this type of tomb may be in Syria or Mesopotamia where many similar tombs have been found. Whether this points to a cultural or ethnic affinity between the inhabitants of Laish and the people further north must await additional research.

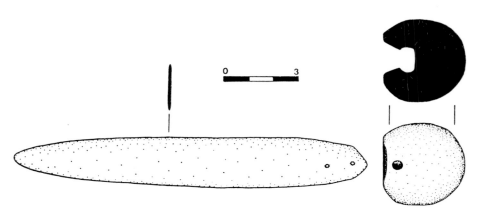

31.   Bronze dagger and pommel from Tomb 1025 (see also Pl. 1)

32.   The stone core in the center of the earthen rampart (Area A)

CHAPTER IV — THE RAMPARTS

The excavations at the ramparts of Tel Dan were conducted throughout many seasons. We attempted to answer three questions: how were they built, when were they built, and who built them? The first indication of the method of construction appeared when we first started the excavations. We found that the southern slope of the embankment was made up of earth gathered by the builders from the remains of former occupational levels. To prevent erosion of the earth-fill sloping at an angle of 38 degrees, a layer of plaster, 15–20 cm. thick, was applied on top of it. The smooth surface and the steep inclination also served to prevent an enemy from climbing the rampart — or at least make it extremely difficult to enter the city. The plaster was anchored by 30–40 cm.-long plaster intrusions into the earth fill. That this was the usual method of construction, was established in subsequent seasons when we discovered these wedge-shaped intrusions in every section of the rampart that we excavated. It is an ubiquitous and easily recognized device, and represents a basic principle in the construction of the ramparts of Laish and other contemporary sites.

The exact width of the base of the rampart can only be estimated. In the excavation of the southern slope we reached a point 24 m. south of the core at an elevation of 192 m. above sea level. This point, however, is not the bottom of the rampart. Because of the later massive stone construction of the Israelite gate here, it was not possible to locate the lowest part of the plastered surface. Considering that bedrock here is at an elevation of 188 m. above sea level, we estimate that the plaster cover starts about 2 m. above that — at 190 m. above sea level. If this is indeed so, the estimated width of the external rampart would be about 27 m. at its base.

The defense of the city was dependent on the outer sloping embankment; its construction required an inner slope and a central core. These we discovered already in the first season of excavations when a 3 m.-high stone construction about 6.5 m. wide, was uncovered. We assumed that it went down much further, perhaps to the level of the foot of the rampart. That would make the core about 10 m. high, and possibly more if it rose beyond the present height of the mound. When we excavated the inner face of the stone core eighteen years later and reached its base, we could determine that it had been preserved up to a height of 10 m. The layers of earth of

33. Barn-owl nest with young at the base of the stone core

the inner rampart were banked up against it. On returning the following year to the exposed core, we found that it had been occupied: a stolid family of barn owls built their nest at the core's base; they came back year after year to raise their nestlings.

The rampart was probably built as follows: At first a core was constructed of rough stones to a convenient height from which earth could be dumped down both sides. The core was then built up higher and more earth was dumped on each side. This process was continued until the desired height was reached and a 38 degree slope was obtained on the outside. The sectional drawing of the southern part of the excavation site shows the stone core in the center and the sloping ramparts covered with plaster on both sides of the core. Since we estimated the base of the outer embankment to be approximately 27 m. from the core, we assumed the dimensions on the inside to be similar. Thus the entire width of the base would be close to 60 m. — a truly monumental building feat of the ancient world. We have now uncovered about 30 m. of the existing surface of the core and no trace of a surmounting wall has come to light.

The pottery found in the earth layers making up the rampart slope is overwhelmingly Early Bronze Age — the 3rd millennium B.C.E., with

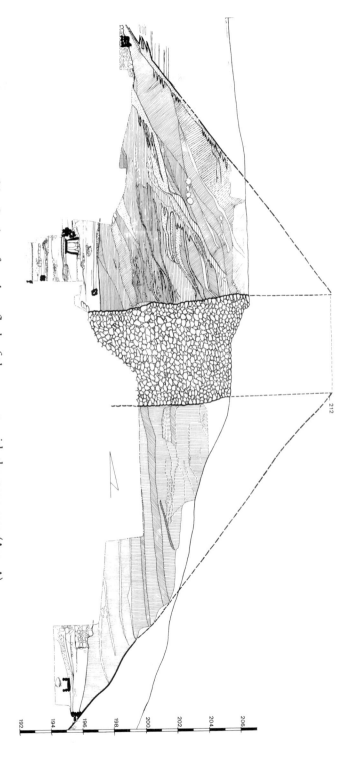

34. Section of southern flank of the ramparts with the stone core (Area A)

some sherds of the Middle Bronze IIA — the beginning of the 2nd millennium. As we have seen, the builders seemed to have scooped up the remains of earlier levels of occupation and used them in the construction of the ramparts. Undisturbed strata appear under the base of the rampart. This means that the ramparts were built at a date later than the undisturbed strata — after or toward the end of the Middle Bronze IIA period. How much later was indicated by the date of the structures and tombs found on the inner slope of the rampart. Since these belong to the Middle Bronze IIB and C periods — the 18th–16th centuries B.C.E., we concluded that the ramparts were built during the Transitional Middle Bronze IIA to IIB period, around the middle of the 18th century B.C.E.

Had the excavations at Tel Dan stopped after the first few seasons we would have assumed that the method of rampart construction described above was followed all over the site. But was it? To answer that question we decided in 1971 to continue our investigation of the ramparts by opening an excavation area at the northeastern edge of the mound — Area Y, which was now free from the threat of Syrian artillery. Since the strategy of narrow, vertical excavation adopted in Area A had proved satisfactory,

35.   Storage jars of the Middle Bronze Age IIA found among the stones of the inward-sloping core in Area Y (see Fig. 22)

it was followed also in Area Y where we opened a trench from west to east, from the top of the ridge downward.

When at the outset of the excavation we encountered a stone structure at the top of the tell, trenching was carried out in two stages: east and westward. The length of the trench to the east, from the top of the mound to the surrounding plain, was about 40 m. In the walls of the trench we could see the layers of the embankment made up of different types of earth, varying in hue from brown-red to brown-black, and orange-colored soil from the river bed containing stones and pebbles of different sizes. Some of the layers of earth were horizontal, although most of them sloped. At the top of the embankment the sloping layers of soil reached to a brick structure 1.7 m. high which was founded on a leveled substructure of fieldstones.

Also in the westward trench we found layers of soil touching the brick structure, but some 50 cm. beneath the level of the fieldstones we uncovered a slope of fieldstones with a 40 degree inclination toward the west. The layers of earth forming the internal slope of the rampart were laid on this sloping stone surface. The upper layer, 1.5 m. thick, consists of brown river-bed soil containing pebbles. Below it is a gray layer about 60 cm. thick mainly of earth from earlier settlement phases. Underneath this layer was yet another one of river sand with stones and pebbles, about 1.1 m. thick. The soil of the embankment did not contain many potsherds, but in the stony slope many finds were made.

Between the fieldstones of this slope, some of which were laid in regular courses and others built in the form of boxed compartments, were pottery vessels, numerous beads and bronze objects. In one jar, in the southern section of the trench, was the skull of a baby. This jar had an oval form with two handles, a flat base and an outward projecting rim with a deep groove through the middle. In other boxed compartments were fragments of a deep cooking pot with a wide shelf rim and a wavy decor scored around the vessel; a flat-bottomed, pear-shaped jar without handles and a grooved outward-flaring rim; and others. This assemblage of vessels found in the sloping stone construction is dated to the Middle Bronze IIA period. The vessels are similar to those found in Area A in the stratigraphic excavation in the southern trench, beneath the rampart. This means that the vessels found here belong to the period before the construction of the ramparts, exactly as in the southern trench. Among the bronze objects were toggle pins, needles, spearheads, and two axes — one, a typical Middle Bronze IIA period duck-bill axe.

The excavations in Area Y continued for several more seasons. About 2 m. north of the trench, we dug down in a square excavation grid area

36. The inward-sloping stone core in Area Y

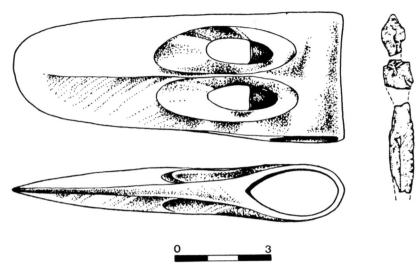

37. Duck-bill axe and fragments of a silver figurine found among the stones of the sloping core in Area Y (see also Pl. 2)

to the stony slope we had discovered in a stratigraphic excavation of the preceding season. In the upper layers of the excavation we came upon pot-sherds from the trench the army had dug before we started work on the tell. Beneath these layers were potsherds of the Israelite period — the 7th century B.C.E. Only below these did we reach the strata of soil belonging to the ramparts, and, after digging 3.5 m. down from the top of the embankment, we came upon the stony slope, which here too inclined toward the west — as we found in the previous trench.

Proceeding with our excavation on the eastern, outer slope of the embankment we found that the sloping layers of soil at the bottom of the trench reached rows of stones. Each row was about 1 m. wide with about 4 m. between the rows. These rows of stones are apparently remains of the Early Bronze period; they were used by the builders of the ramparts as guidelines for depositing the earth for the embankment. At the very bottom of the trench a well-built, 3 m.-wide, sloping wall was uncovered. Its position on the site and the fact that it conformed to the slope of the rampart led us to think that this might be a retaining wall for the rampart. However, Iron Age pottery found embedded among the stones cast doubt on the retaining wall theory. Although the Iron Age pottery may indicate subsequent use of an earlier retaining wall, it seems more reasonable to ascribe the wall to the Israelite period. If so, it represents an intrusion into the rampart material. The outer base of the rampart is here at least 40 m. wide, considerably more than on the south side.

We continued to trace the course of the stony slope at the western trench toward the inside of the mound. About 8 m. from the top of the slope, and 13 m. distant from it, we discovered a leveled surface of stones with a leveled area of earth north of it. This layer was covered with earth from earlier occupational strata containing ashes, broken bricks and many potsherds of the Early and Middle Bronze periods. It was while digging next to the flat stones in order to ascertain whether they were laid on a stone foundation that we discovered the above-mentioned Tomb 1025. Immediately, the question arose whether there is a connection between Tomb 1025 and the stony slope and the earth rampart. From the pottery offerings found inside it, the tomb is dated to the Transitional Middle Bronze IIA–B period, while the objects embedded in the stony slope structure are from the Middle Bronze IIA period. Consequently, the people buried in the tomb lived at a time when the stony slope already existed. Could they have belonged to one of the leading families of the city responsible for the construction of the earthen ramparts? At any rate, the earth layers of natural river-bed gravel and debris of earlier occupation strata cover both the stone structure and the tomb.

The results of the excavation in Area Y indicated that the builders of the ramparts found here topographic conditions different from those in the southern part of the mound, in Area A. Since the builders came upon the stony slope inclining inward it fitted their needs, for they could pile the layers of earth upon it. This however did not resolve the problem of the outer slope of the embankment. They therefore built a 3 m.-wide vertical stone wall (which we exposed to a height of 2.6 m.) onto the eastern face of the stony slope structure. Then, layers of reddish-brown soil brought from the surrounding plain were deposited to form the outer slope up to the level of the original stone structure. Three courses of stones were then laid on the brown earth, forming a platform on which the brick construction of ten courses was erected. The bricks were faced on the outside with stones. The sloping layers of earth on both sides of the brick structure reached its very top, thus forming the steep slopes characteristic of the ramparts built sometime in the middle of the 18th century B.C.E.

Essentially, the method of constructing the ramparts in Area A is identical to Area Y, except for the adaptation to different conditions. For the building of the slope of the rampart the builders needed a central core. To this end they built, at the south of the site, a 6.5 m.-wide stone structure while at the eastern end of the site, where they found an existing stony structure, they apparently did not need to build a wide wall and only added a 3 m.-wide wall with bricks laid on it to form the core structure for raising the embankment.

The excavations of the ramparts at Tel Dan in Areas A and Y seemed to provide sufficient evidence for retracing the method by which they were built. We were determined, however, to avoid a common pitfall — that of over-generalization. All too often, sweeping statements are made about the construction of ramparts throughout the ancient Near East. We wanted to be sure of at least one site — the one we were excavating. Therefore, in 1978, in order to examine the method of rampart construction at Tel Dan once more, we decided to sample yet another part of the mound. To this purpose we opened several small excavation squares at the prominent southeastern edge of the mound — Area K.

The excavation in Area K revealed eight courses of mud brick on top of a flagstone construction, 3 m. wide, sloping westward similar to the sloping stone construction in Area Y. On its eastern, outer side was a 3.2 m. wide earthen mass delimitated by a 60 cm.-thick stone wall. The entire 6.8 m. surface served as a base for the mud-brick construction. The earthen

38.   The core of the rampart embankment in Area K: stone and mud-brick

ramparts abutting the mud-brick structure sloped eastward to the plain below. They consist of layers of red earth which was brought from the river-bed.

On the basis of the excavations in Areas A, K and Y we concluded that the building of the ramparts for the defence of the city of Laish entailed the construction of a central core with a sloping earthen mass on either side. The nature of the central core, however, was different in each of the excavated areas. How different became clear during the excavations in 1989 of Area T.

In this area, on the northern flank of the site, remains of the earthen ramparts had been uncovered in previous seasons. The discovery, in 1979, of mud-brick courses on top of a sloping stone structure appeared at first sight similar to the one discovered in Area Y. However, when we resumed the excavations of Area T in 1988 and 1989, and again in 1991–1992, we realized that while there were here a stone core and sloping earth layers as in the other excavated areas, the core here is strikingly different. The core in Area T is part of an elaborate system including a buttressed wall built of stone with mud-brick on top. Five, possibly six, buttresses or offsets were uncovered, each 2.9 m. long and 1.8 m. wide. The even spacing of 2.2 m.

39. The core in Area T: a complex structure of stone and courses of mud-brick near the top (see also Pl. 5)

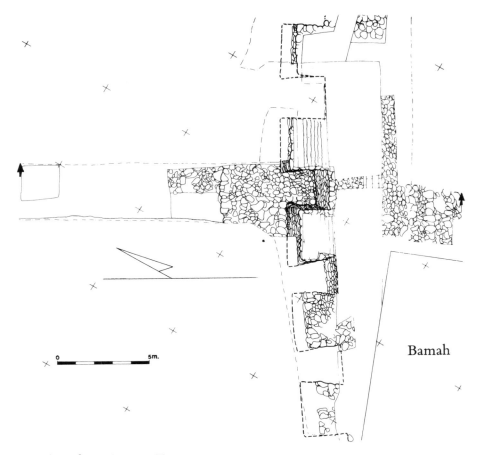

Bamah

40. Plan of core in Area T

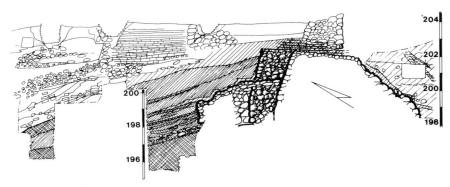

41. Section of Area T ramparts

between each of the buttresses attests to a high level of planning. The buttresses are bonded with the 3.5 m.-wide wall which has now been excavated along 25 m. Two of the buttresses, 4 m. high, were excavated down to their base and appear to have been built on a stone platform. The northern face of the platform was cleared. It is 2 m. high and at its base is a floor of small stones. Between the buttresses is a stone fill extending some 5 m. northward from the wall. This fill, actually a mass of stone, appears to have been laid to support or strengthen the buttresses. It has now been exposed to a length of 10 m. and its face is about 2 m. high. Beneath this stone fill is an east-west, 2 m.-high wall which has been exposed along about 8.5 m. At its base is a surface of small and medium-sized fieldstones. Sloping layers of earth and clay were deposited on the stone fill, the buttresses, and against the bricks at the top, thus forming the outer slope of the earthen rampart. The pottery collected from this slope is mostly Early Bronze with some Middle Bronze IIA. One or two sherds may belong to the Transitional Middle Bronze IIA−B period. Also from this period are several ovens excavated on top of the ramparts. When we excavated the inner slope of the rampart we found layers of earth deposited on a massive sloping stone construction similar to that found in Area Y.

The discovery of this amazing construction of stone and mud-brick raised pertinent questions. Was it built at the same time as the earthen ramparts. If so, why such an elaborate core? If not, was it originally built as one unit or was the stone fill between the buttresses a later addition? In either case could it have been part of the fortifications of the Early Bronze Age? These and other problems still have to be studied. Although at Tel Dan we have probably investigated more of the earthen ramparts than any other excavation, we are only just beginning to understand the complexity of their construction.

That the composition of the material used in the construction of the ramparts is not uniform should not be surprising. The builders used whatever material was most readily available, and the remains of previous strata of occupation were by far the most convenient source and easily transported. The additional earth brought from the surrounding plain contained no potsherds, but the layers of occupation debris provided a large and varied assemblage of broken vessels. These belong mainly to the very large Early Bronze Age city. From that period we have numerous sherds representing a variety of objects already mentioned.

Equally interesting are the material remains from the Middle Bronze IIA period. Early on in the excavation of the inner embankment we noticed a particular class of pottery made of a delicate clay of superior quality from which mostly small bowls and jugs were fashioned. We have variously

42.   Monochrome painted vessels of the Middle Bronze Age IIA and IIB

called it Painted Eggshell ware, Proto-Chocolate ware, Brown-on-White ware, or just "Fine" ware. As these names imply the vessels range from white to yellow to light-pink; they are quite thin and highly burnished. Most of the vessels are painted with fine, brown paint in geometric patterns between metopes. This kind of pottery can be compared to similar ceramics from such sites as Tel Hama, Tel Hadid and Alalakh in Syria. Very little of such pottery has been found south of Tel Dan.

We can only marvel at the planning, execution and labor that went into the construction of these massive Middle Bronze Age ramparts. How many years did it take to build them? That would depend, of course, on the manpower and the time available, i.e., whether there was peace in the land or whether the builders had to hurry the construction because of imminent danger. In any event, we estimate that the construction of the earthen ramparts of Tel Dan — about 1,700 m. in circumference — entailed moving around one million cubic meters of material. Assuming that a workman could move one cubic meter of material per day, it would take a thousand laborers about three years to build these ramparts.

There remains a crucial question. Why build such massive ramparts? There is no general consensus concerning the issue. At Tel Dan especially, one wonders what prompted the people who lived there in the 18th cen-

43.   Bichrome painted vessels of the Middle Bronze Age IIA and IIB

tury B.C.E. to embark on this costly, elaborate construction. The ramparts themselves occupied a fairly large proportion of the site, which considerably restricted the area available for habitation. In other words, by constructing this formidable defense system, the builders confined Laish to remaining a relatively small town with little possibility for expansion. Perhaps topography is part of the answer. Cities located on top of a high hill enjoy natural protection, but Laish of the 2nd millennium B.C.E. had no such advantage and had to find a way to overcome this topographic handicap. Apparently a standard city wall was deemed inadequate, and consequently a mammoth project was embarked upon to create an impenetrable topographic defensive advantage. Some problems however, were not resolved: a way had to be found for draining off excess water from the spring which was now within the ramparts. We did find some evidence for such outlets but could not fully investigate this.

The inhabitants living inside the crater created by the ramparts must have felt safe and secure because of the steep outer slope, and apparently did not think it necessary to build a wall on top of the rampart. The trust the inhabitants had in their mighty ramparts was justified for at least a few hundred years. Only in the 10th–9th centuries B.C.E. did the Israelites erect a city wall at the foot of the outer slope of the rampart, enlarging the city to rival Early Bronze Age Laish.

CHAPTER V — THE TRIPLE ARCHED GATE

Once built, the ramparts were to provide the inhabitants of Laish with a seemingly impregnable defense. But a city must have an entrance and an exit. People went out to cultivate their fields, to trade, to come and go. There had to be gates somewhere in the ramparts. Looking at aerial photographs of Tel Dan taken before the extensive planting of trees took place on the mound, we suspected that there might be a gate in Area Y, somewhat south of our excavation. A probe carried out in the vicinity revealed modern army installations next to what appeared to be the continuation of the Middle Bronze Age stone core. The gate or gates had to be elsewhere and, as is often the case in archaeological research, we discovered the gate quite unexpectedly. The expedition wit likened us to King Saul, who went looking for lost asses and found a kingdom...

In the course of our investigation of the construction methods of the ramparts in Area K, in 1978, we decided to follow the already excavated mud-brick construction in a southerly direction. Some 15 m. further away we came across another mud-brick construction about 30 cm. below the surface. This was not really unexpected, except that it proved to be not the upper part of the core but a well-built wall oriented east-west. During that season (1978), 10 m. of this wall were exposed, and we found that at its eastern end the wall changed direction southward, forming a corner. We traced the new wall in its southerly direction to a distance of 5.3 m. and to a depth of 2.5 m. This was done by removing — actually by peeling off — the reddish soil abutting the wall. Every member of the expedition team joined in attempting to guess the nature of the strange construction that was emerging. As these were the last days of that season's excavation we were left in a quandary as to the true nature of our discovery — was it a new type of Middle Bronze Age core, an isolated tower, a fortress or even, perhaps, a city gate?

When we returned to the site in 1979 and continued carefully to remove the layers of earth, a rectangular construction was revealed and identified as the northern tower of a magnificent Middle Bronze Age gate complex. On the very last day of that season, as we continued to remove the earth that covered the mud-brick edifice, the beginnings of an arch appeared!

How could there possibly be an arch here when we learned at school that

44. Eastern facade of the arched gate entrance to the Canaanite city of Laish (see also
     Pl. 6)

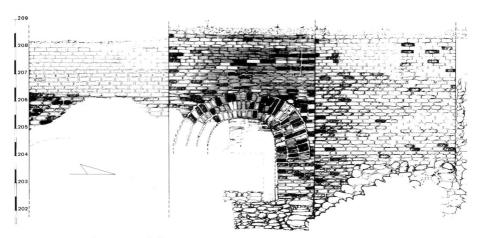

45. Eastern elevation of the city-gate

the arch is a Roman invention? We were surely excavating a city that ante-
dates by two thousand years the Roman occupation of our region! Actually,
it is not quite accurate to say that the Romans invented the arch. We know
of arches in tombs, palaces, and irrigation channels in ancient Egypt and
Mesopotamia. The Romans introduced the use of stone, and with it the
principle of the keystone, and undoubtedly deserve credit for having made
the arch into the characteristic element of their architecture. But here, in
ancient Laish, an arch having a span of 2.4 m. was constructed of sunbaked
mud-brick, three courses thick — some 1500 years before the Romans! Our
imagination ran wild with this discovery, but the answer to our mysterious
arch could be had only after further excavation. We restrained our curiosity
for a whole year until the next season.

Returning in 1980, our strategy seemed simple — follow the mud-
bricks! But the mud-bricks, sunbaked as they were, consisted of the same
material that covered them. There was danger of damaging the bricks even
as we were removing the earth. Fortunately however, the builders of antiquity had coated their mud-brick construction with white plaster which
adhered particularly to the joints between the courses. Patches of this plaster made of lime and calcite were found also on the surface of some of the
bricks. This, and careful work, enabled us to uncover the arch on the eastern, outer face of the construction. We intentionally worked only on the
northern half of the structure in order to minimize danger of collapse and
because we felt we should leave part of the arch untouched for future
archaeological research.

To our astonishment, there was now revealed a gate complex consisting

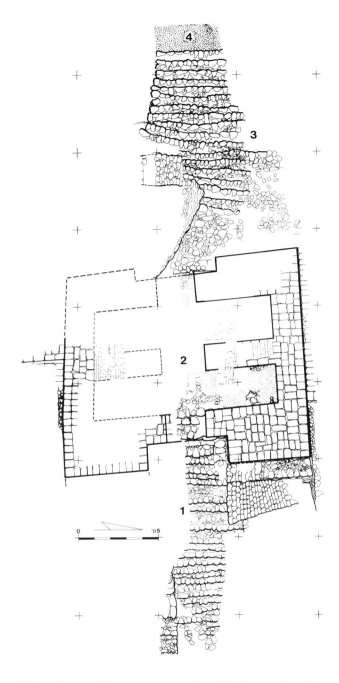

46.   General plan of the triple city-gate area of Laish of the mid-18th century B.C.E.:
       1 — steps leading to the gate; 2 — the city gate; 3 — steps leading into the city;
       4 — street

of two towers each 5.15 m. wide, flanking a recessed arched gateway of the same width. The width of the entire structure is therefore 15.45 m. Some 47 courses of mud-brick were preserved and today the gate stands 7 m. high. Recessed 1.15 m. from the outer face of the towers is the basket arch, with 17 courses of brick above it. The arch is constructed of 3 radial courses of mud-brick 1.25 m.-wide at the spring, 95 cm. at the top, and spanning 2.4 m. The entrance is 3.1 m. high. The approach to the gate from outside the city — from the east — was by stone steps leading from the plain. Twenty steps were cleared along an 11 m. stretch running east. Each step is ca. 40 cm. wide and 10–17 cm. high. Only 3 m. of the width

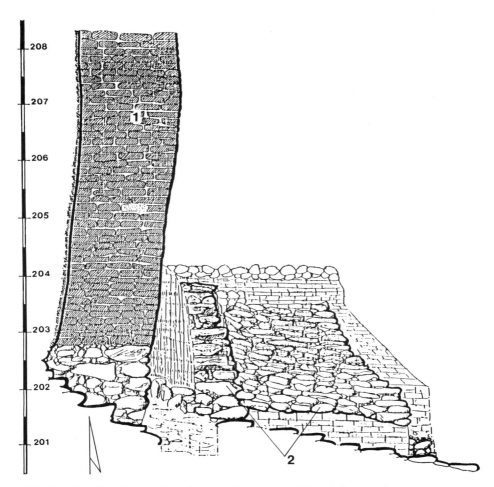

47. Section showing the leaning northern tower (1) and the reinforcing revetment construction (2)

48.   Stepped retaining walls built on to the northeastern tower of the gate

of the entryway was excavated, but we believe it was originally at least 5 m.
wide, the same width as that between the towers. If so, the other 2 m. must
be under the unexcavated rampart material brought later to cover the
entrance to the gate. At the bottom of the steps, a sloping stone pavement
extending a further 2 m. was found, which appears to continue downward
to the plain in a roughly northerly direction. This too is underneath the
unexcavated material.

A probe carried out near the threshold of the gate revealed an earlier

threshold and steps leading to it. Another probe, 5.5 m. east of the threshold, revealed the continuation of the earlier steps about 50 cm. below the
present stone construction. Thus, at least two stages can be discerned in the
construction and use of the gate entrance.

On the north, to the right of the entrance, 14 narrow battered (upward
receding) rows of stone built over mud-brick were uncovered. These were
built against a stone wall, 2 m. high, 1.3 m. wide and extending 5 m. along
the northern tower. We believe that both constructions served as
revetments to support the tower and to prevent rampart material from sliding into the approach to the gate.

Oddly enough, the entrance to the gate was found completely blocked.
The excavation here posed a number of logistical problems to prevent collapse. We decided to dig into the soil blocking the northern half of the
entrance. Starting about 70 cm. from the right doorpost, a 3 m.-long tun-
nel, 1.8 m. high and 1 m. wide was excavated and reinforced with wooden
beams. This was done on the advice of South African mining engineers
who further suggested facing the exposed soil with branches of eucalyptus
saplings. The steps leading up to the gate were found to continue inside.
Three of these were uncovered, the third being 40 cm. higher than the
threshold. At this point we changed course and continued tunneling northward for a distance of 1.3 m. Here we exposed the inner face of the mud-
brick wall of the first pier. The wall still showed traces of white plaster
which apparently once covered all of it.

The excavation of the tower was begun from the surface down and a
square excavation shaft was opened along this inner face of the tower. The

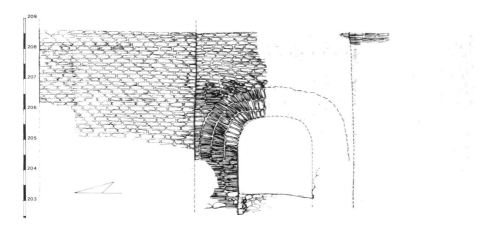

49.   Western elevation of the city-gate from the inside

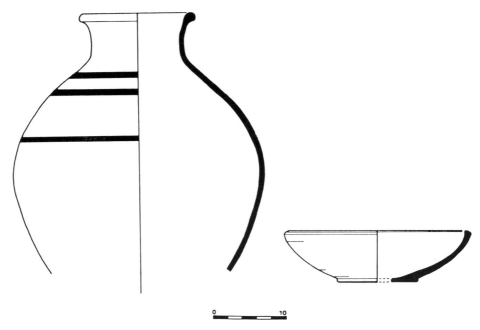

50. Storage jar and bowl of the Middle Bronze Age II A–B found on the floor of
     the gate chamber (Stratum XI)

shaft, 1.75 x 1 m. in cross-section, was excavated by some intrepid volunteers to a depth of 7 m., revealing the north wall and the northeast corner
of a chamber. Remains of white plaster were still visible on the walls. At
the bottom of the shaft, a white plastered floor 10–15 cm. thick laid on
top of a large stone construction was reached. A bowl and fragments of a
storage jar dating to the Transitional Middle Bronze IIA–B period were
found on the floor.

Now we knew that the width of the gate structure was 15.45 m., but
its length had not been determined. We traced 13 m. of the north tower
until we reached a modern road which prevented further work. Consequently a probe was opened on the other side of the road at the place where
we expected to find the exit from the gate into the city. Here we came upon
the same material of which the ramparts were made. At a depth of some
3 m. from the surface, a stepped stone construction was uncovered. This
discovery was puzzling because the construction blocked the presumed
entrance from the gate into the city. We decided to remove the lower rows
of these stones, and as hoped, eventually found steps that led into the Middle Bronze Age city.

When during the course of the following season (1981) we completed

51. Western facade of the city-gate and the steps leading down to the city; note the
     arch at the head of the gate

the excavation of the western facade of the gate complex, an arch similar
to the one in the east was discovered. This one was recessed only 80 cm.
from the outer face of the towers. The length of the passage through the
gate is 10.5 m. and that of the entire structure 13.5 m.

Excavations on the west side of the gate revealed a stone pavement about

3 m. long, perhaps a miniature piazza, which leads from the gate to the first of twenty steps descending westward to a cobbled street 14.5 m. from the gate. The street, 3.25 m. below the level of the gate, continues the descent into the city. Only about 1.7 m. of the length, and 4.4 m. of the width of the street have so far been uncovered. The width of the street and stairway was probably more than the 6 m. of the stairway already exposed. The height of each step varies between 27 and 50 cm.

Another intriguing problem confronted us with the discovery of a battered stone wall situated at the southern side of the entrance, built diagonally northwest for a distance of about 6.3 m. from the entrance. The wall is about 1.5 m. high and appears to abut the corner edge of the archway at the entrance of the gate. Although this did not restrict free passage through the gate, the area of the stone pavement was considerably reduced as a result. Why this peculiar construction? No doubt it was intended to ensure the continued use of the gate. Perhaps in antiquity a structural fault was discovered, or sliding of rampart material endangered the structure. Or it may have served the same purpose as the revetment and retaining wall on the eastern face of the gate where we had noted that the northern tower had begun to tilt.

The construction of the revetments notwithstanding, it appears that the gate was not considered to be safe and ceased to be used. It must have been a well-considered decision: the passageway was deliberately blocked. Soil had to be brought up from the plain and rammed into the gateway and guard-rooms. The entire structure was then covered with earth, the sloping layers of earth on the east and west thus becoming part of the earthen ramparts.

However, a number of questions connected with the construction of the gate remained unanswered: was there a central pier dividing the space inside the gate into chambers? Was the structure roofed? The first question was resolved when we discovered a north-south brick wall which bisected the interior of the gate. The wall is 1.7 m. thick and was found standing to a height of about 4 m. In the middle of this wall we found a third arch. The gate passage through the arches thus divided the gate into four chambers measuring about 4.5 x 2.5 m. each. This arch, like the other two, was built of three courses of mud-brick. However, whereas in the east and west the horizontal mud-brick construction continued for another 2 m. above the arches, we found none of this massive construction above the central arch. Apparently there was no need for it here, for the top of the central arch is level with the top of the wall that was preserved on either side — about 2 m. lower than the top of the gate's exterior walls. The passage under the arches is about 3 m. high in the east, and 2.5 m. in the center

52. The middle arch of the Laish city-gate in Area K (see also Pl. 7)

and west. The northern and southern walls of the gate are 1.85 m. thick, while the walls in the east and west are 3.5 m. and 2.8 m. thick respectively; these dimensions are approximate since the walls were only partially excavated.

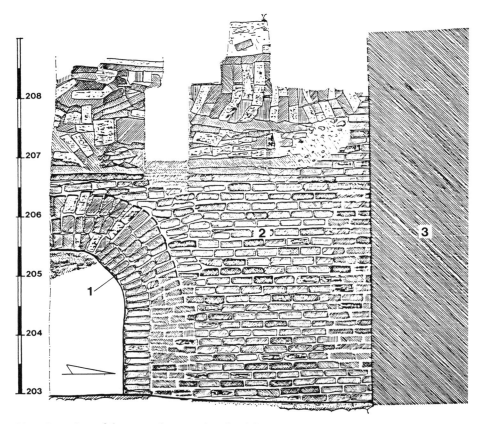

53. Drawing of the central pier and arch of the gate: 1 — the arch; 2 — the mud-brick
     wall dividing the gate structure; 3 — north wall of the gate structure

Was the structure roofed? We believe that the height of the outer walls
of the gate as we found them, about 7 m. above the threshold, is approximately their original height. The central wall, as noted above, is 4 m. high
— presumably the height of the ceiling, since the soil used to block and
fill the gate reached that height. Moreover, the space between the central
wall and the walls to the east and west is about 2.5 m. which could easily
be spanned with cedar beams. The thickness of the central wall (1.7 m.)
is also adequate for supporting such beams. We found no remains of beams
and never really expected to find any: cedar wood was a valuable commod-
ity at all times and would have been removed whenever possible for use
elsewhere. Moreover, since the inner space of the gate was presumably
filled in from above, the wooden beams would first have had to be
removed. There is no indication as to how the beams were attached to the

walls of the gate; perhaps they rested on a wooden frame built against the inner face of the walls. A recess at the base of the mud-brick wall inside the eastern entrance of the gate may have had a structural function, or it may have been connected with the doors, although no additional evidence for doors was found. If our proposed reconstruction of the ceiling and its height is correct, the outer walls of the gate would have extended above the ceiling by at least 2 m. Since in the fill of the gate we found traces of what may be remains of a floor that had been covered by fallen brick walls, the uppermost part of the gatehouse probably continued in use as a large tower in the ramparts fortification system.

The gate, now designated the Triple Arched Gate, was an integral part of the defensive earthen ramparts encompassing the city, and was built

54. The east facade of city-gate complex and towers

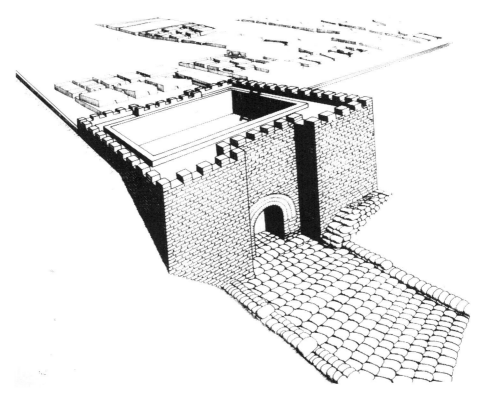

55.   Reconstruction of the city-gate of Laish with the added crenelation

together with the ramparts. The core of the rampart here is 6.5 m. thick
and it is built of masses of brick, stone and earth set side by side. The most
vulnerable part of a fortified city is the gate, and in order to ensure effective
defence it must be situated as high as possible. Today the threshold of the
gate is about 10 m. above the surrounding plain, but geological surveys of
the area show that early in the 2nd millennium B.C.E. the plain was somewhat lower, perhaps by two or three meters. To achieve the desired height
the builders brought soil from the river-bed and erected a narrow artificial
hill, some 12 m. higher than the plain below. This operation was facilitated
by the existence here of an earlier construction, a gate or wall of the Early
Bronze Age. The gate and the earthen ramparts adjoining it were constructed on top of this artificial hill. As the outer walls of the gate were
raised, so was the core of the ramparts. At the same time earth was brought
to build up the sloping ramparts to the north and south of the gate towers.
The outer walls of the gate and the core eventually rose to a height of

7 or 8 m., or approximately 20 m. above the plain; this height and the 40 degree slope of the ramparts provided more than adequate defence.

In order to determine the precise date of the construction of the gate, we examined the composition of the mud-bricks. Most of the sherds found in them belong to the Early Bronze period, indicating what was alluded to earlier, that debris of previous occupation levels was used in making the bricks — just as for the ramparts. The few Middle Bronze Age sherds found also come from earlier occupation levels, as well as from the period when the bricks were actually made. No sherds dated later than the Transitional Middle Bronze IIA–B period were found. The Middle Bronze Age sherds collected from the layers of earth covering the steps also belong mostly to the same ceramic horizon. The pottery found on the floor of the gate provides evidence for dating the last use of the gate. Only few vessels were found here for the gate was not abandoned as a result of violent destruction. When the inhabitants stopped using the gate they obviously removed anything of value. Among the remaining vessels are an almost complete bowl and jar, the lower portion of a jug, and a bowl fragment — all dated to the Transitional Middle Bronze IIA–B period.

After many years of research we have reached the conclusion that the

56. Staff members Hanni Hirsch and Rahamim Goren at work on the preservation of the city-gate

material culture represented in the ramparts and the gate belongs to one homogeneous period — the Transitional Middle Bronze II A–B period, from around the mid–18th century B.C.E. This is the time when the Old Babylonian Kingdom reached the height of its power during the reign of Hammurabi. The contemporary royal archives of Mari tell of strong ties — ethnic, economic and religious — between the West-Semitic elements in Mesopotamia and the people in the western parts of the Fertile Crescent. During this period strong economic ties developed between Mari and such cities as Hazor, some 20 km. south of Laish, and Laish itself. It was a time of extensive urbanization and the later Egyptian Execration Texts attest to the rise of governmental centers. It appears that in most city-states or principalities there was only one ruler. The overwhelming majority of the kings' names are derived from West-Semitic onomastics. This is the period when in Egypt a West-Semitic element had gained a permanent foothold — that would lead to the Hyksos Age of the Second Intermediate Period in Egypt when Asiatics ruled the Nile Delta.

The name of the city, Laish, and its king Horon-ab, appears in the Egyptian Execration Texts. The city received tin sent by king Zimri-lim of Mari. This is also the chronological milieu during which the patriarch Abraham may have spent some time in the city after defeating the kings of the North who took his nephew Lot prisoner (Genesis 14:14). The material culture of the inhabitants of Laish was not radically different from that of the preceding period and does not reflect a change of population. The ramparts and the magnificent gate, perhaps built by Horon-ab himself, reflect the sociopolitical context of the times. Other gates must have served the inhabitants of Laish even when the Triple Arched Gate was still in use, and certainly after it was blocked and covered by earth. Evidence for one such gate, built of stone, was found in 1978 in Area B, in the southern part of the mound.

CHAPTER VI — LAISH DURING THE MIDDLE BRONZE AGE IIB AND IIC

Relatively little information is available about the city of the Middle Bronze II B and C periods. Built within the circumference of the inner embankment, the first Middle Bronze IIB level of occupation in the 18th century B.C.E. (Stratum X) was not larger than 140 dunams (35 acres), with an estimated population of less than 3000. Little is known of these people, for the remains of this early settlement have not yet been excavated. Even in the 2–3 sq. m. that have been exposed in Area M, at the center of the mound, 6 m. beneath the surface, the original Middle Bronze IIB layers of occupation were found to have been disturbed by later tombs and by Israelite silos dug deep into them. Remains of Stratum X were also reached in Areas B and Y at the foot of the slope of the interior embankment. Had the excavation extended toward the center, more information could have been obtained. As is, our knowledge about this and the following period is derived mostly from tombs.

It seems that soon after the ramparts were built the city had to be enlarged, and this could be done in one direction only — up the inner slope of the ramparts. Feeling secure within their formidable defenses, the inhabitants proceeded to construct terraces and houses on the inner embankments. From time to time, tombs were dug under the floors, a characteristic feature of the Middle Bronze IIB and C periods at other sites as well, which provide much information about the people and their material culture.

Two main types of burial were in use in the 18th–16th centuries B.C.E. by the people of Laish — jar-burial of infants and stone-built tombs. Of the latter, some are relatively large, while the small ones are simple cist tombs. Until now twenty-two jar burials have been found, almost invariably under the floors of rooms and courtyards belonging to dwellings, usually next to and at the base of walls. Virtually every excavated room of a Middle Bronze domestic unit contained a jar burial with the remains of a single infant no more than two years of age. In one case we found two infants interred together in a large jar. One very large pithos was found to contain the skeletal remains of a two year-old child (Figs. 62, 63) and a late-term fetus. The position of the skeletons indicates that the deceased must have been inserted into the pithos while it lay on its side. With the

57. Large jar burial *in situ* (Tomb 4648) — Middle Bronze Age IIC
     (Stratum IX)

58. The large burial jar (pithos) after restoration (see Figs. 57; 69:10)

59. Jar burial of infant with offerings *in situ* — Middle Bronze Age IIC, from Tomb 328

60.   Jug and juglets found inside the jar burial (see Figs. 69:3, 12) from Tomb 328

burial was an intact juglet and under the skull of the child and around the bones of the chest area were a number of small, thin spiral shells — perhaps some kind of jewelry or adornment.

Why were these dead infants buried in jars under the floors? The contracted position of virtually all the skeletons and the placement of the head, often at the opening of the jar, may suggest a belief in rebirth, perhaps into the same household. The infants apparently died a natural death for there is no evidence to suggest that the inhabitants of Laish engaged in child sacrifice.

The offerings accompanying the burials vary. In Tomb 328, for example, were three vessels and a scarab; in Tomb 367, only one juglet; while in Tomb 349 were several vessels. These differences in funerary offerings may reflect disparity in the status of the deceased.

The stone-built tombs vary in size and grandeur. The largest is Tomb 4663 which consists of a modest entrance shaft and a large, finely constructed burial chamber. The tomb appears to be an intrusion from a higher

61.   Tomb 4663: the roofing slabs are at the bottom of the picture; above the tomb are layers of the Late Bronze Age settlement, and a storage pit of the Iron Age

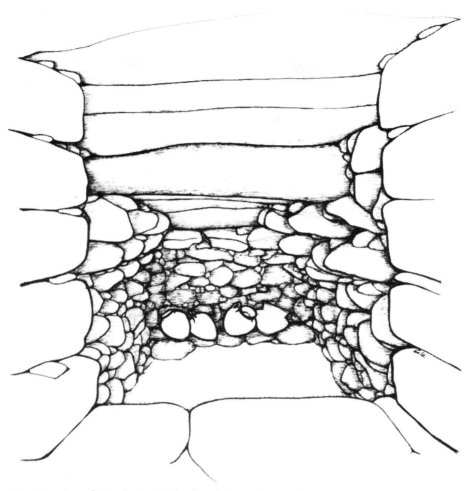

62.   Interior of Tomb 4663, the bench is at the north end

level as a sub-floor tomb. The length of the corbeled construction is about
6 m. and the width and height of the chamber about 2 m. It is built of basalt
fieldstones with travertine stones in some places. Corbeling begins about
half way up the longitudinal walls. The roof slabs laid across the burial
chamber range in length from 75 cm. at the entrance to 1.25 m. The
entrance shaft was found unblocked and led to a step below the threshold.
Along the north wall of the tomb are five flat stones upon which were set
four large, intact vessels: two amphoras, a krater and a carinated bowl.
Other vessels found in this tomb are complete platter bowls with ring bases,

63. Single-handled jars, a krater and large bowl found on the bench in Tomb 4663 (see Fig. 67:9, 10)

lamps, juglets, fragments of Cypriot jugs, a bronze toggle pin or awl, a poorly preserved faience cylinder seal, and a small bone handle. The tomb dates to the Middle Bronze IIB period.

Most surprising about Tomb 4663 is the lack of human skeletal remains. While poor preservation of bone is always something to contend with at Tel Dan because of the high water table, some skeletal material usually survives. Indeed, in many cases animal bones were preserved in quantity. Two possibilities come to mind in explaining what we have called the Empty Tomb. The first is that Tomb 4663 is a cenotaph: a merchant or envoy may have prepared his tomb at Laish but met his end in a distant place. The second possibility suggests that Tomb 4663 was prepared for burial and the offerings deposited in readiness, but for some reason — the most likely suggestion is death in battle — the burial did not take place and out of respect for the deceased the offerings were not removed. The fact that no burial took place may explain the absence of the blocking stone at the entrance — there was simply no need for one.

Tomb 187 was found in Area B, partly in the baulk between two excavation grid squares. Dated to the Middle Bronze IIC period (Stratum IX), it is a rectangular chamber tomb constructed of fieldstones, with rounded north and south ends. It was roofed with long basalt slabs of which three survived *in situ*. Tomb 187 consists of two burials — upper and lower. In the first and lowest burial phase seven individuals were identified. Each had in its turn been disturbed by a subsequent burial. Against the southern wall, six skulls were found with a few other bones, while other bone and skull fragments had been pushed against the eastern wall. A red-slipped and burnished piriform juglet, a large carinated bowl containing a smaller one, fragments of juglets, jugs, bowls, and lamps were found. The upper burial consisted of a single well-preserved male skeleton laid out in a supine position in a north-south orientation, with the head toward the south and flexed legs. A platter bowl was found over the chest of the deceased, a juglet over the abdominal area, a toggle pin over the left shoulder and a carinated bowl at his feet. The significance of the position of these offerings is not clear. The skeletons, as far as could be ascertained, were all males — three mature of over 40 years, two young of 18–20 years, and one 6–year old child.

Another chamber tomb, Tomb 8096, is in a class of its own. Excavated in 1982, it is located in Area M in the center of the city, far from the sloping

64.   Tomb 187 of the Middle Bronze Age IIC (Stratum IX)

65.   Tomb 8096 and offerings *in situ*, Middle Bronze Age IIA–B and until Middle
Bronze IIC

66.   The offerings found in Tomb 8096 (see also Pl. 8)

ramparts. Because of its location, it should have been possible to uncover the buildings and houses occupied by the people buried in Tomb 8096. But the accumulated debris of the later settlements, some 6 m. high, prevented this. Even the existence of an entrance sealed by a rolling stone was confirmed only from inside the tomb. The tomb, measuring approximately 1.5 x 1.5 m., is comprised of a slightly trapezoid burial chamber and a small raised and paved entry passage from the south. A step was laid between the higher floor of the passage and the lower burial chamber. Built of stone, the tomb had a beehive-like corbeled roof closed at the top by a stone slab.

The human skeletal material was found in an extremely poor state of preservation and had been disturbed in antiquity by successive burials, rockfalls and burrowing animals. Hence the number of interments is unclear and may have been greater than the five individuals identified. The earliest burials were those of a mature male aged 30–40, a female aged 18–21, a juvenile about 5–7 years old found between them and a juvenile aged 8–12. The skeletal remains were probably moved from the center of the tomb together with the accompanying burial goods to make room for subsequent burials. Traces of corroded metal on the arms and ribs of the mature male may have come from a sword that was found nearby. The scarabs, bronze weapons, toggle pins and fragments of alabaster vessels belong to the earliest burials. The later burial of a female aged 30–40 was in the center of the burial chamber and near the entry passage. Judging from the finds of the Transitional Middle Bronze II A–B period it appears that the tomb was originally built then. However, the majority of the finds are to be dated primarily to the Middle Bronze IIC period.

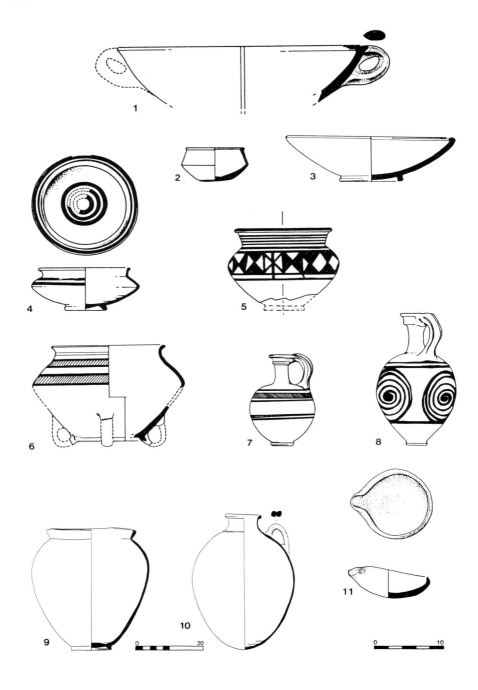

67. A selection of Middle Bronze IIB pottery: 1–6 — bowls; 7, 8 — juglets;
9 — krater; 10 — jar; 11 — oil-lamp

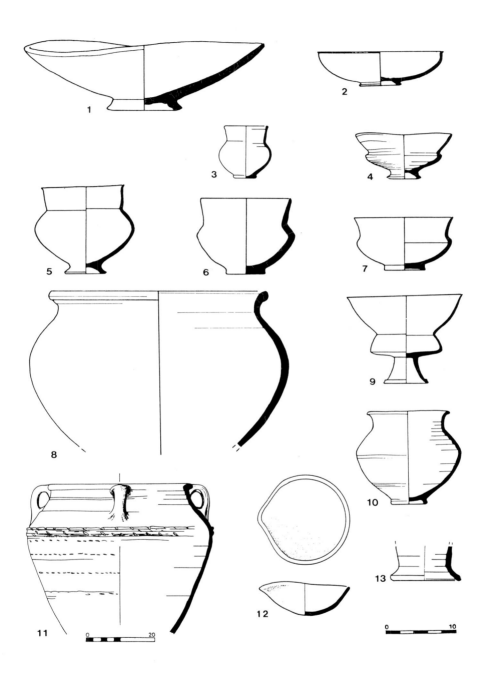

68. Some of the vessels of the Middle Bronze Age IIC: 1–7, 10 — bowls;
     8 — cooking pot, 9 — goblet; 11 — krater; 12 — oil-lamp; 13 — stand

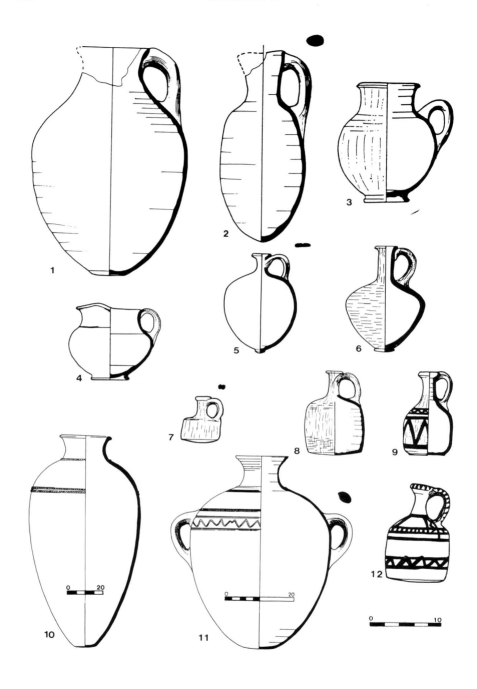

69. Pottery vessels of the Middle Bronze Age IIC (Stratum IX): 1–4 — jugs;
     5–9, 12 — juglets; 10 — pithos; 11 — jar

70.   Reconstruction of cosmetic box with bone inlay from Tomb 8096

After the last interment, one of the large roof slabs apparently collapsed, perhaps in an earthquake, blocking a section of the burial chamber and part of the passage. The Cypriote Base Ring jug and the platter bowls of the Late Bronze I may represent the continued tradition of a particular family leaving offerings at the tomb of their ancestors.

The Middle Bronze IIB and IIC periods were apparently times of peace and prosperity. From the examination of the animal bones, we can conclude that the inhabitants enjoyed a mixed diet based on hunting and herding. Various species of deer were hunted. The domesticated animals were goats, sheep, cattle and pigs. Among the bones were also those of a donkey and a dog. The increase in population called for additional housing which now reached the upper part of the slope. The inhabitants undoubtedly needed public buildings, palaces and temples. These are probably located in the as yet unexcavated areas. The cultural material remains represent a rich, cosmopolitan civilization that ended in a violent conflagration.

Already in the 1968 season the floor of a room was uncovered in the northeast portion of Area B, with a number of vessels in a 30–50 cm.-thick layer of ash and destruction. The vessels, which belong to the end of the Middle Bronze IIC period, help date the fire that consumed the building. We considered that the destruction may have been the result of one of the Egyptian campaigns of the 16th or 15th century B.C.E. — perhaps that of Ahmose I or Thutmose III, but could not determine whether the evidence of the 1968 season pointed to a total destruction of Laish at that time. In the subsequent seasons however, layers of destruction were discerned in Areas M and T below the Late Bronze Age strata, and in 1986, we excavated a new square in Area B some 20 m. west of the square uncovered in 1968, where an almost identical thick accumulation of conflagration debris was found. We may thus reasonably assume that at least one of the Egyptian pharaohs destroyed Laish in his advance northward against the kingdom of Mittani. Laish, however, did not stay long in ruins. Soon after, the Late Bronze Age dawned bright with promise.

CHAPTER VII — LAISH IN THE LATE BRONZE AGE

A large krater dated to the beginning of the Late Bronze Age was found in 1969 near part of a wall, high up on the inner slope of the rampart. This suggested that around the 16th–15th century B.C.E. the city had expanded beyond the boundaries of the previous settlement. Then, in the 1988 season, a massive stone construction of that period was uncovered on the same slope, some 40 m. to the west, lending further support to our original conclusion.

Late Bronze Age remains of the 16th and 15th centuries B.C.E. (Late Bronze I) were found in practically all of the areas excavated. The vessels from the beginning of this period clearly showed continuity from the previous one, except that at this stage a new type of painted vessel made its appearance. This pottery is painted in red, or red and black, directly on the clay or on a pale-colored slip. Such bichrome ware appears in the 16th century B.C.E. and is also common at the beginning of the 15th century B.C.E. The nature of the structural remains could not always be determined. However, one building, excavated in Area K at the southeastern corner of the mound, was of particular interest. It is located some 18 m. west of the Triple Arched Gate on top of the mass of earth covering the Middle Bronze Age street. So far, 9 m. of the building's eastern wall and 8 m. of its southern wall have been exposed. The walls, built of fieldstones, are 90 cm. thick and are preserved to a height of 1.5 m. The building is divided into two sections by a pier integral with the southern wall. The eastern third of the building was paved with large flagstones. To the west of the pier the floor was of pale-colored beaten earth. The finds include the butt of a bronze javelin, a limestone mold (for casting bronze maceheads or scepter heads?), and several vessel fragments all dated to the Late Bronze I. The function of the building is not clear; could it have been a temple? A female pottery mask, painted mostly white with the eyes and eyebrows emphasized in dark brown, that was found among the collapsed stones of the building may perhaps have some cultic connotation.

A surprising find made in the 1986 season of excavation in Area B shed some light on the activities of Late Bronze I Laish. It was the discovery of a crucible with bronze slag and a well built furnace full of ash. Already in previous seasons we had discovered an extensive area of metal workshops

71.   Clay mask found in collapsed Building 6156

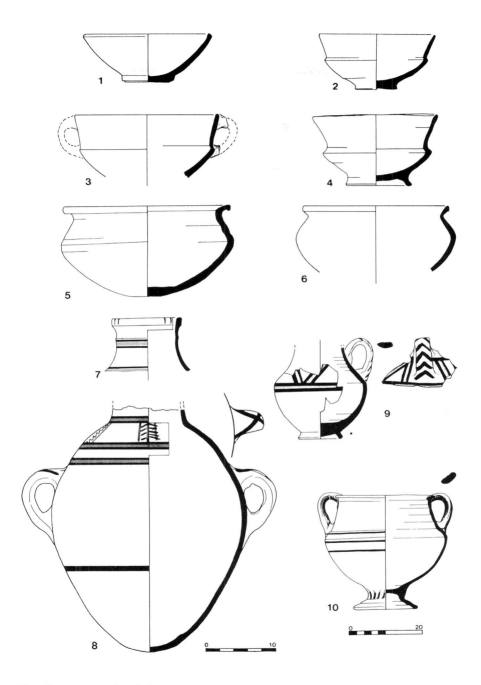

72. Pottery vessels of the Late Bronze Age I: 1–4 — bowls; 5, 6 — cooking pots; 7, 8 — jars; 9 — jug sherds with bi-chrome decoration; 10 — krater

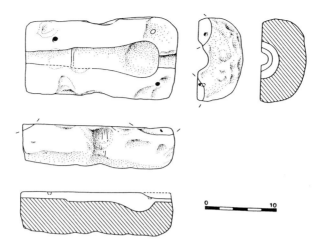

73.   Stone mold, Late Bronze Age I (see also Pl. 11)

of the Iron Age or Israelite period. Now we had evidence for a metal work-shop some 350 years earlier. The implications of this discovery will be dis-cussed in Chapter IX.

The circular wall of the furnace was made of clay. To ensure stability and preserve heat, sherds from broken pottery vessels were laid against the outer face of the furnace. When these sherds were collected and restored they formed two vessels — a decorated chalice and a carinated bowl — both classic Late Bronze I vessels. The dating for the crucible and furnace — the second half of the 16th century or first half of the 15th century B.C.E. — was supported by other artifacts in this area. Some 15 m. further west, a room was found with a number of Late Bronze Age vessels. In another room under the stone floor a jar burial of a four-week-old infant was found. J. Zias of the Israel Antiquities Authority, who did the anthropological analysis of this jar burial, found that along with the human remains were those of an adult sheep. According to him, while grave offerings of a sheep or a goat are common to Canaanite mortuary practice, the inclusion in an infant jar burial is unusual — if not unique.

Despite the paucity of material available from this period, sufficient evi-dence has come to light to indicate that the Late Bronze Age I was a time of growth, development and cultural exchange. No evidence for the destruction or abandonment of Late Bronze I Laish (Stratum VIII) was encountered in the course of the excavation. The Late Bronze II city (Stra-tum VII) that followed continued very much like its predecessor and if the

74. Kiln of the Late Bronze Age I (Stratum VIII)

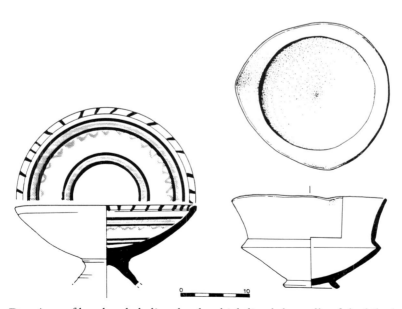

75. Drawings of bowl and chalice sherds which lined the walls of the kiln (see also Pl. 12)

76.   Bilbil — imported Cypriote jug (see Fig. 82:3)

discovery of Tomb 387 is any indication, it was considerably more prosperous and cosmopolitan.

Tomb 387, named the Mycenaean Tomb after the numerous imported Mycenaean vessels it contained, was discovered accidentally, as so often happens during an excavation. This occurred during the 1969 season when we sought to determine the nature and date of the Middle Bronze Age earthen ramparts. We had uncovered the plastered surface of the inner slope of the ramparts in Area B and decided to trace it. We wanted to reach the lowest point of the incline where we could expect to encounter the level of occupation contemporary with the rampart construction. We hoped at that level to obtain conclusive evidence for the date of the ramparts as well as information about the people who lived within them. However, this ambitious plan had to be abandoned when in the last week of that season a narrow, 2 m.-long stone wall bordering a stone floor was revealed. The discovery there of a bilbil juglet — an imported Cypriot type — pointed to a Late Bronze Age II date for this construction. When the skull of a man and several leaf-shaped arrowheads were found on the stone floor we concluded that this was a Late Bronze Age tomb.

The discovery of Tomb 387 called for a change in excavation strategy. Our original plan to try and trace the course of the inner ramparts had to be postponed. Instead, we decided to concentrate on excavating the immediate vicinity of the tomb. In order to examine the relationship between the tomb and its surroundings, and excavate the tomb itself, we extended the area under investigation and opened two new grid squares on the surface of the mound. In this way we hoped to obtain the complete sequence of occupation of the site in this area, and to determine the various stages of use of the tomb. The latter goal was especially important in establishing the relative sequence of the burials in the tomb and the offerings which accompanied each burial. We soon realized that our hopes would be only partially fulfilled. The upper layers, about 1 m. thick, had been badly disturbed by later burials, and as for the tomb itself, the roof had collapsed in antiquity causing considerable damage to the burials and offerings. Moreover, the earlier burials had been pushed aside to make room for later ones, causing disorder in the skeletal remains and offerings. This precluded obtaining a clear stratigraphic and chronological sequence of the burials and their respective vessels. The tomb and its contents had to be studied as one archaeological entity.

Tomb 387 — the Mycenaean Tomb — was dug into the earthen layers of the rampart's inner slope, under the floor of the Late Bronze Age residential structures, some 18 m. north of the stone core. The tomb is built of rough stones and two of the walls are preserved to a height of 2.3 m.

77. Tomb 387 of the Late Bronze Age II (Stratum VII)

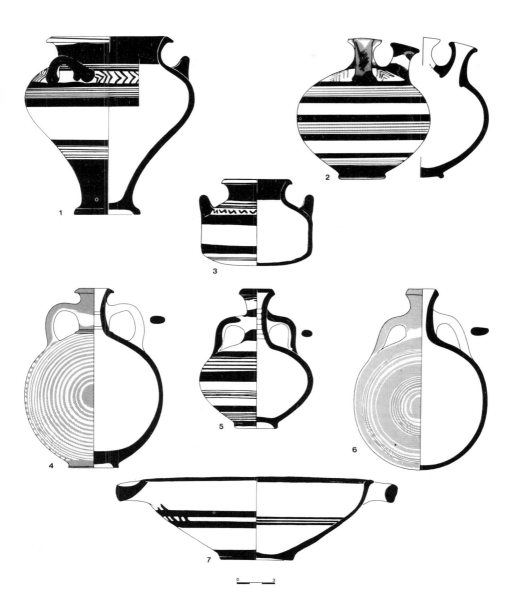

78. Vessels imported from Mycenae found in Tomb 387: 1 — piriform amphoriskos; 2 — stirrup jar; 3 — pyxis; 4–6 — pilgrim flasks; 7 — bowl (see also Pl. 13)

— very possibly the original height of the tomb. The north and south walls are corbeled to support the slab roof. The floor is made of flagstones and measures 2.2 m. in the west, 1.9 m. in the east, and 2.45 m. on the north and south sides. We were unable to find the entrance, but it was probably to the west, at the northwest corner of the tomb chamber — a common phenomenon in contemporary tombs at Ugarit in Syria and at Enkomi in Cyprus. There too, these tombs were found within the confines of the domestic quarters. The remains of the roof, made of large slabs, had collapsed inside the tomb and potsherds of the Late Bronze II period were found in the fill above the collapsed roof. Inside the tomb were the remains of some 40 skeletons of which 25 could be identified as males, 9 as females and the remaining 6 of undetermined sex. The ages vary from one 60 year-old man to a child of 5. Most of the deceased belong to the 25–30 year age group. The anthropological examination by B. Arensburg of Tel Aviv University revealed that among the people buried in Tomb 387 were some who anthropologically did not belong to the local Canaanite population. The origin of this foreign element remains a mystery.

The accompanying burial offerings were numerous, varied, and unusually rich — altogether 491 items! These included 108 pottery vessels, 2 alabaster vases, 4 basalt bowls, a perfectly preserved bronze oil-lamp, an

0   1

79. Hathor scarab in the form of a frog from Tomb 387; left — upper side, right — bottom

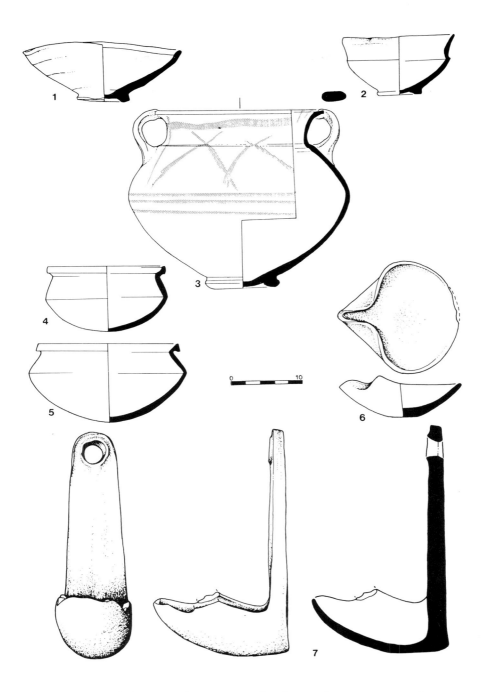

80. Pottery vessels from Tomb 387: 1, 2 — bowls; 3 — krater; 4, 5 — cooking pots;
6 — oil-lamp; 7 — hanging oil-lamp fixture

almost undamaged bronze censer, a bronze bowl with an animal-shaped handle, 5 other bronze objects, about 83 weapons — among them 3 daggers and one decorated spearhead, 3 cosmetic boxes made of hippopotamus tusk, a miniature box made of a deer antler, a relatively large amount of bone and ivory inlays, 30 gold and silver pieces of jewelry, faience and glass vessels, beads, a (Cypriot?) stone cylinder seal depicting a griffin and a horned animal, and a Hathor scaraboid in the shape of a frog — perhaps an amulet. One-hundred-and-ten spindle whorls of stone, bone, ivory and one of metal were found, as well as various metal objects probably used as nails and needles. Also found in the tomb were olive pits, and on the floor, the bones of a sheep. Of the 108 pottery vessels, 14 were intact specimens and 94 were restored, providing a total of 96 complete vessels. Of this assemblage, imported vessels constituted about 30 percent of the total, 2.8 percent being Cypriot and 26 percent Mycenaean imports. The Cypriot imports included a bilbil and two bowls — one a "milk bowl" and the other a Base-Ring II type. Among the Mycenaean imports were exquisite stirrup and piriform jars, alabastrons, pyxides, flasks and bowls, and a unique "charioteer vase" — the first complete example found south of Ugarit. Neutron Activation Analysis by J. Gunneweg and I. Perlman showed that the charioteer vase, as well as other Mycenaean vessels, were made in the Argolid in Greece. These belong to the late Mycenaean IIIA2 or early IIIB period, dating to the second half of the 14th century B.C.E. and the early 13th century B.C.E. It was these impressive import wares that led us to dub Tomb 387 the Mycenaean Tomb and to suggest, partly in jest, that it was the family mausoleum of the ambassador of Mycenae to Canaanite Laish. The imported cylinder seal may lend some support to the possibility that the tomb indeed represents the interment of a government official.

The local pottery repertoire consists of 25 jugs, 17 flasks, 13 bowls, 7 oil-lamps, one wall-bracket used as a stand for an oil-lamp, 7 cooking pots, 3 kraters and 4 storage amphoras which laboratory tests showed to originate from the Phoenician coast. The number of storage amphoras is relatively small, and the typical Late Bronze Canaanite "commercial" storage amphoras, so common in the country's Late Bronze Age tombs and structures, are absent — as are dipper juglets which are usually found in quantities in tombs and structures of the period in Israel. Aside from these peculiarities the repertoire in Tomb 387 of Laish is similar to those in other Late Bronze Age II tombs found elsewhere in the country.

Although the Mycenaean Tomb remains the most impressive discovery of the Late Bronze Age at Tel Dan, later excavation seasons revealed much more of Laish in the 14th–13th centuries B.C.E. and of its highly developed material culture. Above the occupation levels of the Late Bronze I

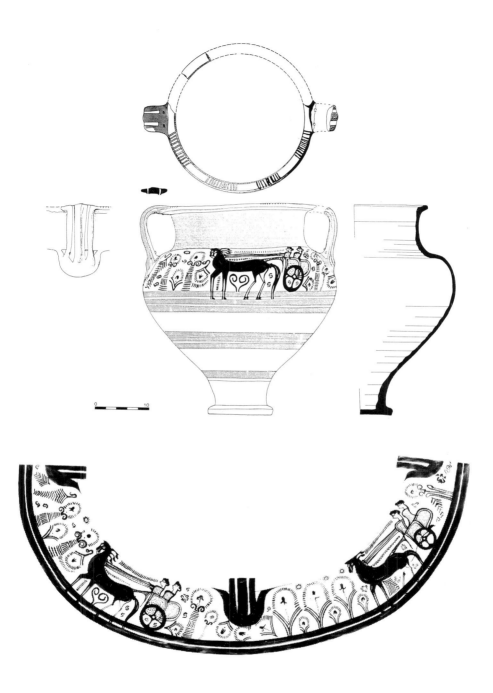

81. Mycenaean charioteer vase from Tomb 387 (see also Pl. 17)

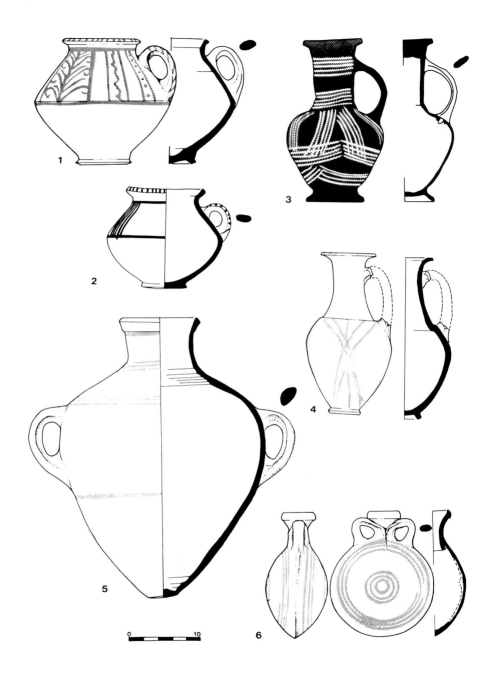

82. Additional pottery vessels from Tomb 387: 1, 2 — biconical jars; 3 — Cypriote
     bilbil; 4 — local imitation bilbil; 5 — jar; 6 — lentil-shaped pilgrim flask (see
     also Pl. 18, 19)

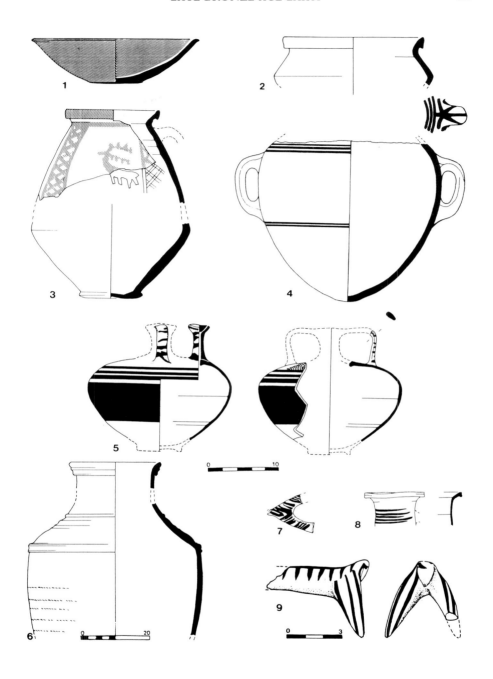

83. Vessels of the Late Bronze Age II (Stratum VII): 1 — bowl; 2 — cooking pot; 3 — biconical jug; 4 — jar; 5 — Mycenaean stirrup jar from Area Y; 6 — Hazor-type pithos; 7, 8 — fragments of Cypriote milk-bowl and bilbil; 9 — zoomorphic figurine, Mycenaean import

in Area B, a large flagstone floor was uncovered, bordered on the east by a massive stone wall, while in the northwest was a stone circle with two upright stones at one end. A molded clay plaque depicting a man playing a lute-like instrument and his right foot raised as if dancing was found about 10 cm. below the surface of the pavement, where some of the flagstones were missing. The plaque may have belonged to the people who built the flagstone pavement in the 14th century B.C.E. We promptly called it in rhyming Hebrew *ha-raqdan me-dan* — The Dancer from Dan. This plaque is of special interest. The lute was a common musical instrument in antiquity and is found on numerous ancient plaques and paintings. Representations of both male and female dancers are also known, but a male dancer of such elegant movement as portrayed on the plaque from Dan is remarkable. The grace and freedom of our dancer are especially significant. He wears a kilt similar to the ones seen on Hittite plaques and other examples from Mesopotamia and north Syria. His strange facial expression may represent a mask. It is a tempting speculation that the Dancer from Dan belonged to a guild of performers in the Canaanite city of Laish in the 14th–13th century B.C.E. Perhaps the flagstone pavement was a courtyard where dancing and singing took place in cultic celebrations. Music and dancing have been part of human culture from time immemorial. In biblical tradition Yuval, the father of all players of the lyre and harp, is counted among the ancestors of mankind; the prophets accompanied themselves on musical instruments, and King David is described as dancing before the Ark of the Covenant being brought to Jerusalem (2 Samuel 6:16; 1 Chronicles 15:29).

Both the Mycenaean Tomb and the Dancer from Dan were found in Area B of the excavations as was most of our information concerning Late Bronze II Laish. Here a number of rooms were uncovered containing vessels typical of the period. However, important Late Bronze Age finds also come from the other excavated areas. An Egyptian scarab of Rameses II was found on a floor in Area Y and, on another surface close by, rested a number of Late Bronze Age vessels including a decorated Mycenaean stirrup jar. Remains of a large building were uncovered in Area M above Tomb 8096, as were large Canaanite pithoi of the 14th–13th century B.C.E. in Area T. Unfortunately most of the evidence of the latter part of Late Bronze II Laish has disappeared, being destroyed in the course of building and leveling in the 12th century B.C.E. and subsequently. Thus little can be said of the nature and character of the settlement that preceded the arrival of the Tribe of Dan. The pottery vessels found are typical of the period; characteristics of the previous period and signs of a process of degeneration can be distinguished — as in the carinated bowls. Especially noteworthy

84. The "Dancer from Dan" — Late Bronze Age, Area B

85.   Scarab of Rameses II from Area Y

are pilgrims' flasks covered with a white slip painted with concentric circles; the wide variety of cups and jugs, both regular and biconical; and
amphoras decorated with metopes and geometric patterns, and even with
the deer motif which is a common filler pattern in this style. Particularly
significant is the presence of imported wares from Greece, Mycenae and
Cyprus, and their imitations. These point to extensive commercial relations and cultural influences that characterize all of the Late Bronze period.

86. Bones of a fallow deer and potsherds on Late Bronze Age II floor of room

CHAPTER VIII — "AND THEY CALLED THE NAME OF THE CITY DAN"

One of the most complete accounts of the migration of an ancient Hebrew tribe recorded in the Bible is in the Book of Judges, Chapter 18. Read together with Joshua 19:40–48 and Judges 1:34 the story unfolds as follows: Originally Dan was to occupy a territory along the course of the brook Sorek and the hill country of the northern extremity of the Judean Shephelah and around the Valley of Ayalon. Unable to gain a foothold in its allotted territory, the tribe moved north, conquered Laish and changed its name to Dan. On the way, the tribe collected cultic vessels and a priest from the land of Benjamin. The graven image, ephod, teraphim (Judges 18:20) and mask were then probably set in a sanctuary. The priests, descendants of Moses, "were priests to the tribe of Dan until the day of the captivity of the land", i.e., until the Assyrian conquest. The "graven image" however, lasted only "all the time that the house of God was in Shiloh" (Judges 18:31), i.e., the middle of the 11th century B.C.E.

We do not know whether the whole of the tribe migrated north and took part in the conquest of Laish. The Bible mentions that six-hundred armed men of the family of the Danites set forth (Judges 18:16), but does not tell us by what strategy they conquered Laish. The description of the people of Laish as being "quiet and secure" reflects, possibly, the faith of the indigenous population in what they assumed to be impregnable defenses. Living behind their great earthen ramparts the Canaanites must have believed that no enemy would be able to scale these and conquer Laish. The date of the conquest of Laish by the tribe of Dan has long engaged the attention of biblical scholars and historians, but there is no consensus. When we began the rescue excavation of Tel Dan, we wondered whether archaeological evidence would introduce a new objective element into the discussion, and help resolve the issue. A datable conflagration layer could, for example, relate to the account in Judges 18:27 if taken literally: "and they smote them with the edge of the sword and burnt the city with fire". On the other hand, Joshua 19:47 does not mention fire. We hoped for tangible evidence from the excavation to determine a date for the settlement of the tribe. Perhaps our findings might even allow us to suggest which of the two biblical accounts reflect more accurately what actually happened.

The flagstone pavement in Area B of the Late Bronze II (Stratum VIIB), dating to the 14th century B.C.E., was found with a 1 m.-thick layer of collapsed mud-brick on top of it. This collapse represents the destruction of the buildings associated with the flagstone pavement. Above the collapse, poorly preserved remains of walls and structures were found. According to the ceramic evidence, these belong to an occupation level or settlement of the 13th century B.C.E. and constitute our Stratum VIIA. When, some 20 m. further east, the remains of structures built when Tomb 387 was no longer in use were excavated, we also found this layer of occupation. A thin layer of destruction by fire could be discerned above these structures. A similar layer, representing a moderate degree of destruction, was observed also in other grid squares excavated in Area B. Perhaps this thin layer of burnt material and ash relates to the mention of the destruction of the city in Judges 18 and in Joshua 19.

Subsequent discoveries in Areas T and K provided more information on the transition between the Late Bronze and Iron Ages. At the northern end of the site in a small probe in Area T, we found a number of pottery vessels on a floor covered by a thin layer of destruction by fire. The vessels include 3 chalices, part of a krater on which is painted the likeness of a bird, a storage jar and rims of cooking pots. These vessels, still made in the Late Bronze Age tradition, are also indicative of the beginning of the Iron Age, and are dated to around 1200 B.C.E. In Area K, in a conflagration layer we found 2 bowls and a storage amphora also belonging to the transition between the Late Bronze and the Iron Age around 1200 B.C.E. To the same period belong a flask and a pyxis found on the southern edge of the mound in Area B. All these finds are from a phase of occupation heralding the beginning of the Iron Age but still bearing vestiges of the Late Bronze Age. While we cannot definitely say which phase actually represents the last Canaanite city of Laish, it is reasonable to assume that the destruction layers described above belong to it. However, we are quite certain of the next level of occupation, Stratum VI.

The archaeological excavations in many parts of the site now revealed a total change in the character and material culture. The most striking feature of this change is the appearance of a large number of deep storage pits found in dense clusters all over the site. They were first noted in the initial seasons of excavation, and we discovered more and more of them as we continued working — particularly in Area B. Dug into the debris of earlier strata of occupation, the pits vary in size, depth and method of construction. Some of them are lined with stones, some are dug into a layer of gravel

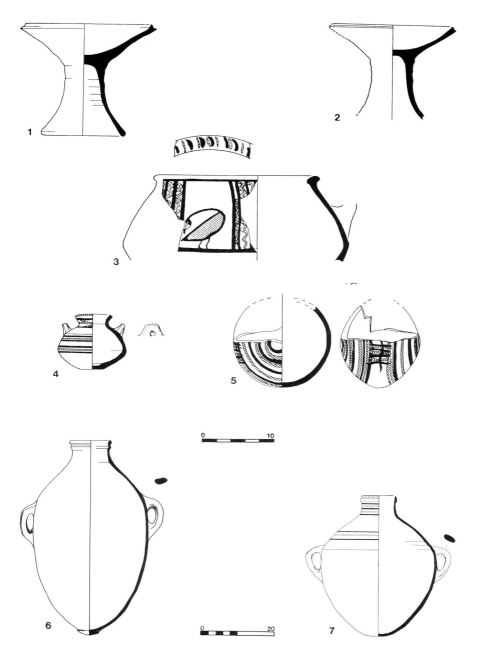

87. Pottery vessels representing the transition from the Late Bronze to the Early Iron
      Age: 1, 2 — chalices; 3 — krater; 4 — pyxis; 5 — pilgrim flask; 6, 7 — jars

and still others are not lined at all and could not be easily distinguished. The appearance of the pits suggests not only the end of one stratum of occupation and the beginning of another, but also — and more significantly — a radical change in the settlement pattern and life-style of the inhabitants to the point of implying a change in population. It does not seem reasonable to suppose that the people of the Late Bronze Age, who enjoyed a sedentary and relatively high level of urban culture, would suddenly abandon their way of life and adopt a mode of living more suitable to a nomadic or seminomadic society. The latter, a mobile people, living in tents and huts, would require a large number of pits for storage. It seems therefore that the changes which took place express the advent of a new people accustomed to a nomadic or seminomadic life.

The contents of the pits revealed a material culture markedly different from that of the Late Bronze Age described in Chapter VII. Mycenaean and Cypriot imports now no longer appear in the ceramic assemblages, and

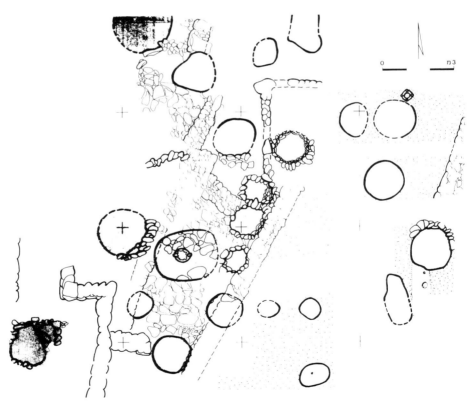

88.   Plan showing location of pits in Area B (Stratum VI)

89. Two of the pits in Area B (Stratum VI)

the local ware is characterized by the appearance of large amphoras and pithoi. When the fragments of pithoi were restored into complete vessels, we wondered if they had been intact or already broken when deposited in the pits. It seemed reasonable to suppose that the pits were originally intended for use as storage silos, especially for grain. The pithoi, on the other hand, while also serving as receptacles for grain storage, were used primarily for liquids — oil, wine and water. It is likely that some of the pithoi might have been placed in a pit for better protection. In any case, the appearance of the pits and of the pithoi in Stratum VI clearly indicate a population whose economic and social organization required ways of storing large amounts of food, both solid and liquid.

When, in 1974, the first pithos of Stratum VI was discovered in Pit 1225 we were not surprised that it was a "Galilean" type pithos, a typological descendant of a northern Canaanite pithos common in the Late Bronze Age and found mostly in northern sites such as Hazor and Tel Dan itself.

90.   Pit 1225 with 12th century B.C.E. pithos fragments (Stratum VI)

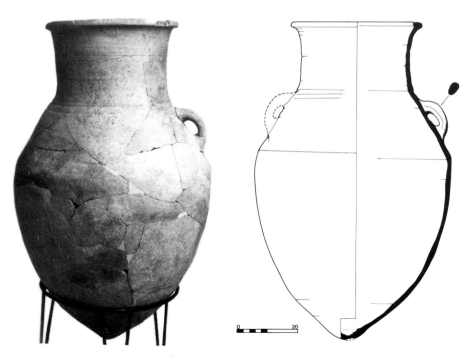

91.   "Galilean"-type pithos from Pit 1225

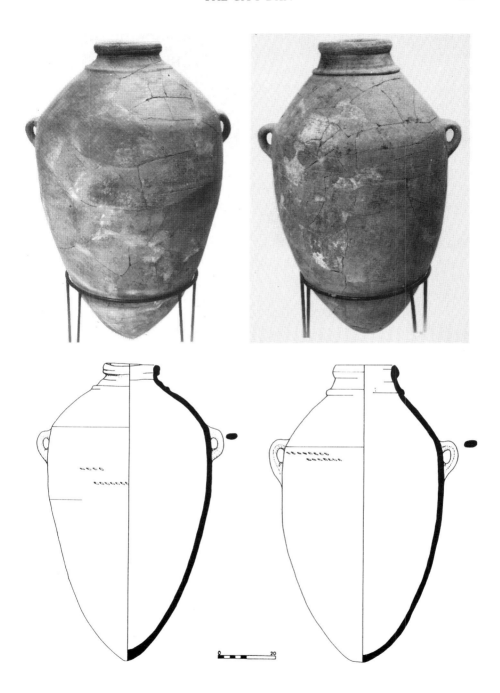

92.   Two collared-rim jars from Pit 4349 (Stratum VI)

Pottery-making traditions do not cease abruptly, but persist also after new techniques and new forms are introduced. What was surprising was the discovery, in the same pit, of the upper part of a large vessel with a distinctive rim belonging to a type called collared-rim jars. We were already aware of the existence of collared-rim jars at Tel Dan. They had appeared early in our excavation in Stratum V in a thick layer of destruction dated to the mid–11th century B.C.E., but this was the first indication that their appearance at Dan may be dated earlier. That this was indeed the case was confirmed when more collared-rim jars, many of them complete, were subsequently found in Stratum VI. In fact, it turned out to be the dominant pithos type in this level. The significance of the collared-rim jars appearing in such large numbers in Stratum VI, the first level of occupation following the Late Bronze Age, cannot be underestimated. The implications for outlining the settlement history of the site soon became apparent.

It was W.F. Albright who first suggested in the 1930s that the collared-rim jar is connected with the settlement of the Israelites in the land of Canaan. This theory has been contested, but collared-rim jars are indeed found in large numbers precisely in Israelite settlements, especially of the hill country. At Tel Dan the collared-rim jars appeared in the pits dug into the levels of the Late Bronze Age city. This strongly suggests that they were not indigenous to the area, but were introduced to the site by a new group of inhabitants. Given the biblical evidence, the obvious candidate is the tribe of Dan. Moving from the coastal plain through the hill country, the Danites were either already acquainted with this particular type of jar or had adopted it in the course of their migration. That the jars discovered at Dan were not identical was to be expected. Such jars could not be exactly the same since the body was made by hand and the neck on the potter's wheel. Moreover, they were apparently made in different localities. The results of the Instrumental Neutron Activation Analysis carried out by J. Yellin and J. Gunneweg of the Hebrew University have shown that some of the collared-rim jars were made locally at Dan while others originated from different parts of the country.

Our conclusion that Stratum VI with its storage pits represents a population whose material culture and mode of living was unlike that of the earlier inhabitants is also supported by the study of other pottery vessels found in the pits. Many of the pottery types in this stratum constitute a connecting link in the development of ceramic wares of the Late Bronze Age and the Iron Age. They also exhibit new departures. Thus, for example, bichrome decoration which was common in the previous period now appears in a degenerate form; the Mycenaean and Cypriot imported wares disappear. In addition to the expected range of pottery vessels such as jugs and juglets,

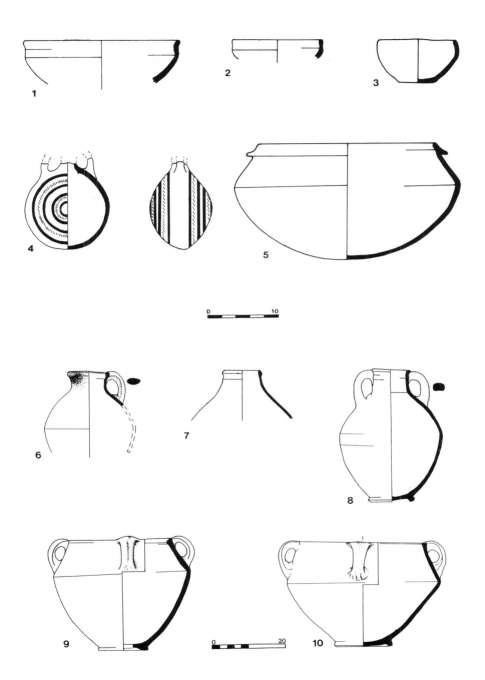

93. Iron Age I pottery vessels from Stratum VI: 1–3 — bowls; 4 — pilgrim flask;
5 — cooking pot; 6 — jug; 7 — jar; 8 — amphoriskos; 9, 10 — kraters

small bowls, flask and pyxides, what also distinguishes Stratum VI is the number of large kraters and cooking pots. Together with the large storage jars, these vessels point to their use by a typical seminomadic society made up of clans and large families. Once again, the 600 men of the tribe of Dan making their way from Zorah and Eshtaol and camping on the way come to mind. As the Book of Judges 18:12 tells us, they "pitched in Kirjath-jearim...wherefore they called that place Mahaneh-dan...." i.e., the camp of Dan.

If we are right, then the first phase of the Israelite settlement at Tel Dan, Stratum VI, represents the migration and settlement of the tribe of Dan and the conquest of Canaanite Laish. Assuming that the smaller potsherds found in the pits are the discarded, broken vessels of an earlier phase, while the complete vessels belong to the last phase when the pits were in use, we would date the beginning of Stratum VI to the first half of the 12th century B.C.E., coming to an end in the third or fourth quarter of the 12th century B.C.E. The latter is the date of the complete cooking pot found just a few centimeters below the rim of Pit 1225 which is almost 2 m. deep. This new period, marked by pit and silo construction, belongs to the Early Iron I (or Israelite I) period and it is to this — the first half of the 12th century B.C.E., possibly the first quarter — that we would also date the settlement of the tribe of Dan in Laish. After conquering Laish "...they called the name of the city Dan, after the name of Dan their father...." (Judges 18:29), the name by which it would henceforth be known.

How many Danites settled in the newly conquered city? We are told, in Judges 18:11 and 16–17, that 600 fighting men sallied forth from Zorah and Eshtaol. We are also told of small children, sheep and goats, and various belongings. Presumably there were also men and women, young and old, and babies, accompanying the men of war. Assuming (at a calculated guess) two fighting men per family, some 300 families, or 1500–2000 persons may have reached Dan. Such a population could easily be accommodated in the area conquered and made available for settlement within the confines of the ramparts. Of the physical and anthropological characteristics of the Danites, now settled in their new quarters, we know nothing. No skeletal remains of these early Danites have been found. Indeed, no skeletal remains at all of the Israelite period have been discovered at Dan until now. Apparently, in keeping with Israelite custom, the deceased were not buried under the floors of dwellings but in an ordinary cemetery somewhere in the surrounding fields at the foot of the mound. Only if their remains ever come to light it will be possible to add the physical anthropological aspect to this research.

We also know very little about the early Danites' livelihood once they were settled. The animals they brought with them would be put to graze in the lush pasture of the land. Animal bones found in the pits of Stratum VI were mostly of goats and sheep with some cattle — a pattern characteristic of seminomadic pastoral transhumance societies. Also found were the bones of a gazelle, bird and a dog. It appears that the Danites owned some cattle in addition to large herds of sheep and goats. The domestic animals provided a diet of meat and dairy products, and secondary products such as wool and hair. This was supplemented by venison of gazelle, fallow deer and roe deer from the slopes of Mount Hermon and the river valley. It was not necessary to go far afield to hunt these animals. The bones that were examined were from both fat and lean parts, which suggests that entire carcasses were carried back to the settlement and consumed there. Fresh-water fish-bone and mollusks also found in the pits give an idea of the varied diet enjoyed by the early Danites.

Situated as it is on a main crossroads, ancient Dan may well have exacted a toll from the caravans passing through the area. Possibly this is alluded to in the blessing of Jacob "Dan shall be a serpent by the way, an adder in the path..." (Genesis 49:17). If the boats mentioned in the Song of Deborah (Judges 5:17) refer to boats on Lake Hula, the Danites may also have engaged in limited watercraft. Of one of their occupations we are certain — the Danites were metal workers (see Chapter IX).

About their religious practices we know only what we are told in Judges 18. It appears that in their original territory around Zorah and Eshtaol the Danites had no priest or oracle to guide them. The five Danites who were sent to spy out the land sought and received God's blessing from the priest they found in the house of Micah in a village in the hill country of Ephraim. It also appears that the tribe lacked any ritual utensils or paraphernalia, such as those they took forcibly from the house of Micah. And they had to persuade the priest to accompany them to their new abode and to become their spiritual leader. This priest, a grandson of Moses, established at Dan the priesthood that served the community for over 400 years.

It did not take the tribe of Dan long to shed its seminomadic character. Our next level of occupation, Stratum V, represents an urbanized community. We know that Stratum V ended in a violent destruction of the entire city. In every excavated grid square we found evidence of fire and everywhere the debris lay over 50 cm. thick. The fire that destroyed the houses also burnt the reeds in the ceiling, traces of which could be discerned in the collapsed remains of the roof. The destruction of the city of Stratum V was apparently the result of complacency. The Danites too, like the people of Laish before them, put their trust in their mighty ramparts. No evidence has so far been found to indicate that the Danites had settled outside

94. Pottery fragments from burnt level of Stratum V

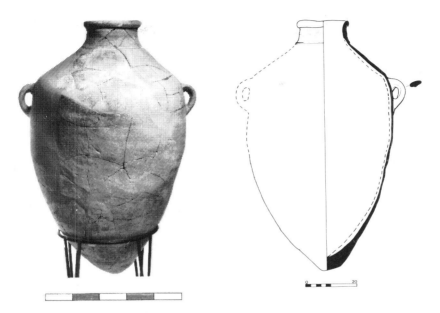

95. Collared-rim pithos from Stratum V

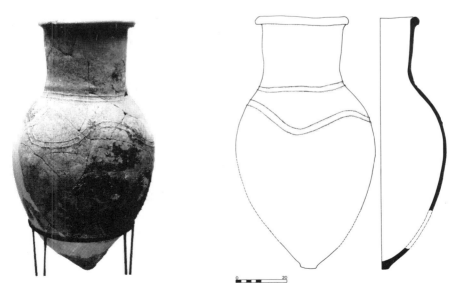

96. Phoenician-type pithos

the perimeter of the ramparts, or that they built any other fortifications to defend their city. What enemy could overcome the rampart defence system? After a peaceful existence of some 100–150 years, it must have seemed inconceivable to them that what had happened to the Canaanites of Laish could also happen to the Israelites of Dan.

The study of the pottery found in the destruction level points to a date around the mid–11th century B.C.E. This is also the time of the destruction of Shiloh by the Philistines. The reference to that disaster in the last verse of Judges 18 testifies to the impact the removal of the Ark from Shiloh had on the people of Israel, even as far as Dan, who recall it when describing the calamity that befell their shrine.

The material culture of Stratum V belongs to the same cultural milieu as that of Stratum VI. Two phases of occupation, Dan VA and Dan VB, could be discerned in the city built over the pits of Stratum VI. Although

97.   Reed impressions from clay ceiling that collapsed in conflagration in Stratum V

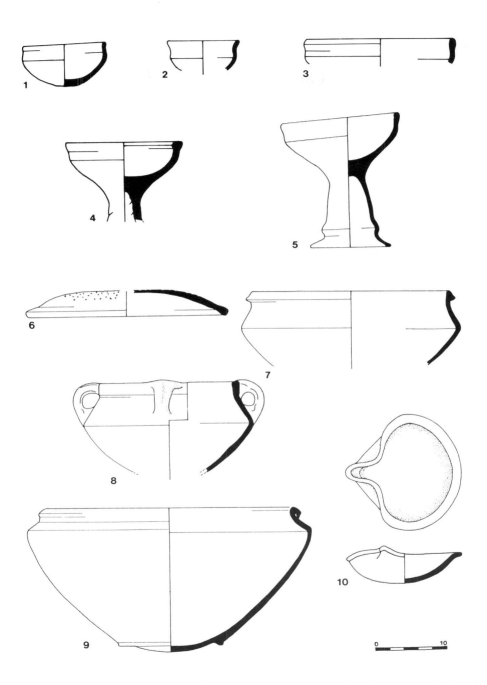

98. Iron Age I pottery vessels from Stratum V: 1–3 — bowls; 4,5 — chalices;
    6 — baking platter; 7 — cooking pot; 8, 9 — kraters; 10 — oil-lamp

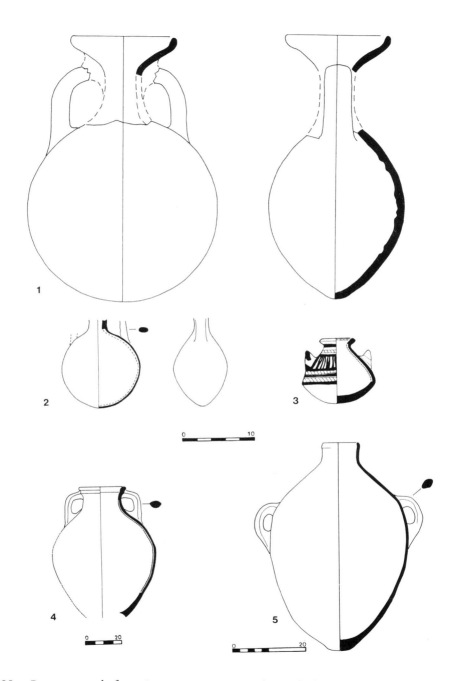

99.   Pottery vessels from Stratum V: 1, 2 — pilgrim flasks; 3 — pyxis;
      4 — amphoriskos; 5 — amphora

100. Pottery vessels from Pit 3127 representing Strata VI and V

the walls of the houses remained the same in both phases, separate floor levels could be distinguished. The pottery vessels of Dan V are very much the same as those of Dan VI — after allowing for minor changes in form that naturally occur in the course of a few decades. But there are two typical exceptions. The first is the appearance of a new "Phoenician" type pithos so called because it is found on the Phoenician coast. This type of pithos is also found in the settlements of the Galilee hill country. The Phoenician pithos, unlike the Galilean and collared-rim pithoi, is completely hand-made. An incised, wavy decoration, which may be traced originally to Cyprus, runs around the jar. The second typological difference between Dan V and Dan VI lies in the larger number and greater variety of small vessels in relation to the larger amphoras and pithoi. Many jugs, juglets, small and large bowls, chalices, flasks and pyxides were found and it seems as though the inhabitants, having adopted a more sedentary existence, could now indulge in the luxury of acquiring vessels elegant as well as practical. To this period we ascribe the Philistine sherds found inside a large jar in a stone-lined pit in Area Y. Two of the sherds are of the classic, fine Philistine bichrome ware, while the third is part of a locally made krater

101. Head of clay figurine from Area T, Stratum V

decorated with a Philistine motif. In Area T a unique decorated figurine head was found in the Dan V destruction level, but its cultural origin has not yet been determined.

Whatever caused the downfall of Dan V and its destruction in the mid–11th century B.C.E., it did not result in the abandonment of the site. The city was soon rebuilt, ushering in our Dan Stratum IV. The houses retain the walls and plans of the former Dan V settlement. Only in a few places were new walls built, dividing the spacious areas of Stratum V into smaller units, and perhaps indicating a more intensive, crowded occupation. The finds from these houses include amphoras, cooking pots, chalices, pyxides and oil-lamps.

At least two phases were discerned also in Dan IV. In Stratum IVB — the second half of the 11th century and the first half of the 10th century B.C.E. — the ceramic tradition of Stratum V is evident in most pottery types. But the collared-rim jar, so prominent in earlier Israelite strata, had disappeared forever. The Galilean and Phoenician pithoi, while still in use, were apparently no longer essential to the life of the community. It is as

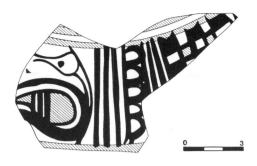

102.   Philistine sherds and locally-produced decorated krater from Stratum V (and see
       also Pl. 20)

though the need for large storage vessels had changed, for we now find
the more manageable smaller storage jar most prevalent. In this level
appears a new element — Phoenician bichrome (two-colored) jugs and
flasks decorated with concentric circles or with bands around the body. The
finds from the dwellings include jars, cooking pots, chalices, pyxides,
lamps, and jugs with red and yellow slip decoration and burnishing. A
wealth of large and smaller bowls, also with yellow and red slip decoration
and burnishing, many of them carinated, were found mainly in the open
areas of Stratum IVA. Assemblages of slip-decorated and burnished ware

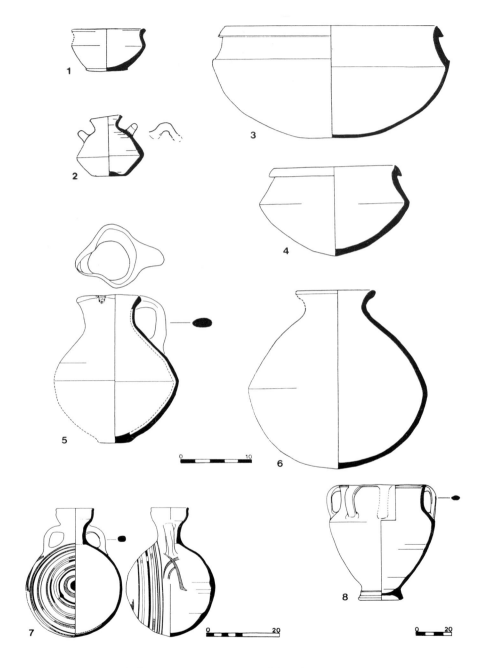

103.   Pottery vessels from Pit 3127: 1 — small bowl; 2 — pyxis; 3, 4, 6 — cooking
       pots; 5 — jug; 7 — pilgrim flask; 8 — krater

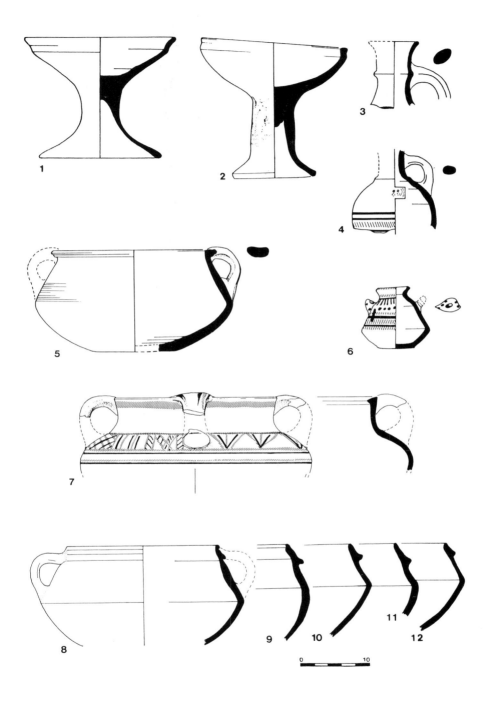

104. Pottery vessels from Stratum IV: 1, 2 — chalices; 3, 4 — jugs; 5, 7 — kraters;
      6 — pyxis; 8–12 — cooking pots

appear for the first time in the second half of the 10th century B.C.E. in Dan and at other sites in the kingdom of Israel, and they are very common throughout the 9th century B.C.E. Another pottery group that makes its first appearance in the second half of the 10th century B.C.E. comprises Cypriot-Phoenician juglets in red and black.

The end of the 2nd millennium and beginning of the 1st was a period of consolidation and expansion of Israelite territory under the United Monarchy. In the days of King Saul, Dan may have been part of the district of the Asherites (2 Samuel 2:89). King David fought the Arameans and his writ reached Damascus and beyond. As related in 2 Samuel 24:6, his census of the population began at Dan. Solomon, the great merchant king, controlled the trade routes, and Dan, situated on the main roads, must have enjoyed economic prosperity. Among the twelve administrative districts under Solomon (1 Kings 4:15), Dan was part of the ninth district, but under the name of the tribe of Naphtali rather than that of a city. It was but natural to include Dan in the district of Naphtali, since tradition held that both were sons of Bilhah the handmaiden of Rachel (Genesis 35:25). Also in Deuteronomy 27:13, in the account of Israel becoming a people on the mountains of Ebal and Gerizim, Dan and Naphtali are mentioned together. Following the death of Solomon and the division of the kingdom, Dan was the place where Jeroboam the son of Nebat set up one of the golden calves (1 Kings 12:28–29). The stage was now set for the emergence of Dan as the major religious, administrative and military center in the north of the country.

Bronze dagger and pommel
from Tomb 1025

1

Duck-bill axe from Area Y

2

Beads found between stones of
the core in Area Y

3

Fragments of silver figurine
from Area Y

4

5

Stone and mud-brick structure serving as a core for the ramparts in Area T

6

View of the eastern
facade of the Middle
Bronze Age city-gate

7

The middle arch in
the city-gate of Laish

The offerings from
Middle Bronze Age
Tomb 8096

8

Jar burial *in situ*

9

Juglet found in the
jar burial

10

Stone mold of the Late Bronze Age I and a modern scepter-head cast in it

11

The vessels which lined the kiln of the Late Bronze Age I, after restoration

12

Imported Mycenaean
vessels found in
Tomb 387

13

Gold jewelry from
Tomb 387

14

Cosmetic box made
from deer antler, from
Tomb 387

15

Bronze bowl with
handle depicting an
animal (calf?) from
Tomb 387

16

17

The charioteer
vase from
Tomb 387

18

Imported
Cypriote bowls
from Tomb 387

Pilgrim flask from
Tomb 387

19

Philistine sherds
and a local
decorated krater

20

Crucible and
tuyère (blowpipe)
found together
in Area B

21

Ferrules of spear
butts found in
the metal
workshop areas

22

Objects found in
the workshop
areas

23

Bronze figurine of
female warrior in
smiting pose

24

Seven-spout
oil-lamp

Bowl with
bar-handle and a
trident incised on
its base

25

26

Head of a figurine
found on the pebble
floor

Incense stand found
on the pebble floor

27

28

29

30

Faience figurine of a
king or deity holding a
lotus stem

Faience figurine of
monkey

31

Head of faience
figurine of an Egyptian
king

Bronze and silver
scepter-head found
under the stones of the
altar

32

Three iron shovels
found near the altar

Bronze bowl found near
the altar

33

34

35

Remains of a structure in
use until the Persian
period

Figurine in Egyptian-
Phoenician style

Faience die

36   37

Figurine of the god Bes

Bronze figurine of Osiris

38

39

Head of female figurine

40

Oil-lamp of the Roman period

41

Decorated amphoriskos

42

Two pithoi of the
7th century B.C.E.
from Area T *in situ*

43

Base of the
canopied structure

44

CHAPTER IX — THE METAL INDUSTRY AT DAN

Perhaps the term industry is too presumptuous, but then we may be excused for being carried away in our enthusiasm when, in 1974, the first indication of metal working came to light at Dan. In Area B (Stratum IV) we discovered an almost complete crucible with bronze slag clearly visible inside a small stone installation. Nearby were parts of the clay pipes through which air pumped from the bellows reached the furnace. The crucible and blowpipes (or tuyères) were found in a level of occupation dated by the cooking pots, chalices, small bowls and bichrome jugs to the end of the 11th–beginning of the 10th century B.C.E., corresponding to Stratum IV at Dan. In the course of the following season, in 1975, more parts of crucibles and blowpipes were found some of which came from an earlier occupational level. We concluded at the time that this was evidence of the Danites engaging in metallurgy. The verses in 2 Chronicles 2:13–14 came to mind, in which Hiram the king of Tyre tells King Solomon that the mother of the artisan sent to help in the building of the Temple is of the "daughters of Dan". We interpreted this statement to mean that the king of Tyre, who wanted to impress Solomon with the artisan's qualifications refers to the fact that he hails from Dan, a place with a long tradition of metallurgy.

A few more years passed before the excavations revealed just how extensive was the metal working activity at Dan. In 1984, at the southern end of Area B, a crucible was found upside down within a circle of stones. This installation is also dated to the 11th century B.C.E., as were the earlier ones. However, a furnace discovered in 1985 showed that the Canaanites of Laish were already engaged in metallurgy in the Late Bronze I period. Did the Danites learn the trade from the Canaanites or did they already possess this knowledge when they came north?. The metallurgical analysis carried out at Tel Aviv University by S. Shalev showed that the mineral composition of the slag and metal of the two periods were not the same, and this complicated the picture. The question still stands — even though in the 1986–1988 excavation seasons we learned much more of the Danites' metallurgical activities, and better understand the various stages and processes of this technology.

In the 1986–1988 seasons a metal workshop dated to the beginning of the Israelite period was found in Courtyard 7026 and in the surrounding

105.   Crucible from Stratum IV in Area B found in 1974

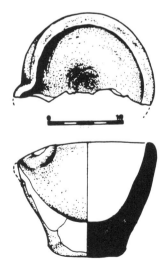

106.   Drawing of the crucible found in 1974 (see also Pl. 21)

107. Metal-working installation and crucible found in 1984

108. Remains of the metal workshop in Courtyard 7026 (Stratum VI)

109.   Remains of the metal workshop in Courtyard 7061 (Stratum V)

rooms, at the southern entrance to the city, close to the ridge. Two circles of stones, parts of crucibles (one almost complete), bronze slag, basalt tools, and parts of a pithos and of pottery vessels were found. A pithos sunk into the ground was of the collared-rim type, and around it were parts of crucibles, slag, and sherds of various vessels which included chalices, jugs and cooking pots. North of Courtyard 7026 we uncovered a furnace built of the fragments of a cooking pot. Also found were a number of hearths which contained ashes, crucibles, blowpipes and remnants of metal.

The finds in Stratum VI, which include grindstones, a metal blade, an ivory handle, jugs, storage jars, chalices and cooking pots are from the beginning of the 12th century B.C.E. It stands to reason that when the Danites first settled on the ruins of Canaanite Laish, metallurgy was already one of their major pursuits. That such work was part of their tribal background may be deduced from the reference to Oholiab, son of Ahisamach of the tribe of Dan, who helped in the building of the Tabernacle (Exodus 31:6, 35:34, 38:23).

In the next occupational level in Stratum V, the remains indicate more extensive metal workshops. Two circular installations made of stones, crucibles and blowpipes were found encompassing a relatively large work area (No. 7061). From the sherds lining one of the installations (No. 7068) we

110.   Vessels from Room 7082 *in situ* (Stratum V)

111.   The vessels from Room 7082

were able to restore an almost complete cooking pot. In between and under the stones forming the installations, the end of a blowpipe integrated into the furnace was found *in situ*. On the floor was a large amount of ash, slag, hematite stones, beads and animal bones the color of oxidized copper. Nearby were smoothed basalt stones for use in the workshops, sherds of pithoi, chalices, crucibles, stands for offerings and slag. In a room to the east of the courtyard, a complete crucible, cooking pots, kraters, a bowl and animal bones were found.

Of unusual interest were the finds in a small room (No. 7082) measuring

1.5 x 1 m. On the plaster floor were parts of crucibles, basalt pounders, a chalice, a krater, a bowl, a jug, and a remarkable vessel in the shape of a house identified as a "snake house" because of its similarity to such vessels from earlier periods found in sites such as Ugarit in Syria and Hazor to the south of Dan. Many more vessels were found in other rooms in this area. These included trefoil pinched-mouth jugs, a decorated pyxis, numerous flint, limestone and basalt tools, and many other vessels all belonging to Stratum V of Dan. Stratum V begins in the latter part of the 12th century B.C.E. — a generation or two after the conquest of Laish, by which time the seminomadic tribe had turned sedentary. It is tempting to see in the large number of chalices and in the snake house evidence for cultic practices associated with the metal industry. In such a case, the snake house may well have been modeled after a temple.

One of the puzzling aspects of this metal industry was the absence of objects made there. Nor for that matter were any molds found, apart from one made of stone excavated in Area K in a Late Bronze I building. The friable clay molds probably disintegrated in the course of time. As for the bronze objects, the 1988 season provided part of the answer. To the circular

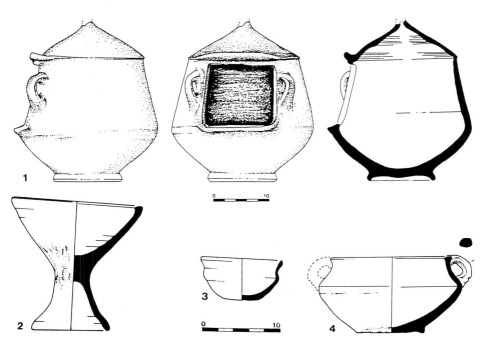

112.   Drawings of vessels from Room 7082: 1 — "snake house"; 2 — chalice; 3 — small bowl; 4 — krater

113.　Vessels from Room 7063 near Room 7082

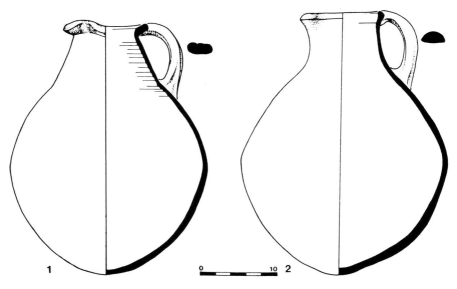

114.　Jugs found in Room 7063

installations already known was added a square one containing a crucible and a bronze object. Also uncovered that season were shallow pits 1 m. in diameter that may have been hearths. Besides a relatively large quantity of ash, we found slag, parts of crucibles, bronze needles, an unfinished copper axe, an unidentifiable bronze object, a large number of flint tools, and two bronze objects — probably spear butts, although they may have been agricultural tools. It appears that the Danites used discarded and broken metal objects for the production and repair of agricultural and other tools.

The fate that befell the city of Dan of Stratum V also affected the area of the workshops. As in the other excavated areas, here too a layer of destruction and ash was found above the installations and the room with the snake house. As mentioned, this destruction did not bring about the abandonment of the site, and in the industrial area the houses were soon rebuilt reusing the same walls, while adding new courses and raising the levels of the floors. Many finds were made here: crucibles (some complete), slag, large vessel fragments, large chalices, a bichrome flask, an incense cup and many other vessels. One of the special items is the fragment of a wing and head of a bird (a duck?) — part of a ritual chalice similar to others found in Tell Qasile in the Philistine Stratum X. This was the last phase in the metal industry found in Area B, and is dated to the end of the 11th-beginning of the 10th century B.C.E.

The concentration of the metal workshops in Area B at the southern part

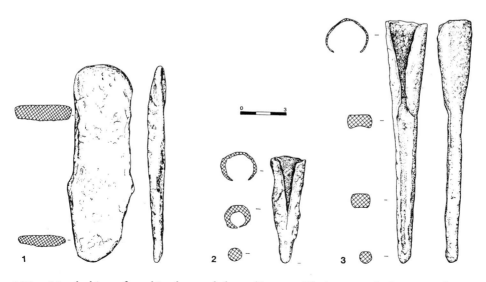

115. Metal objects found in the workshops (Stratum V): 1 — axe; 2, 3 — spear-butt ferrules (see also Pl. 22)

116.   Finds from Stratum IVB workshops

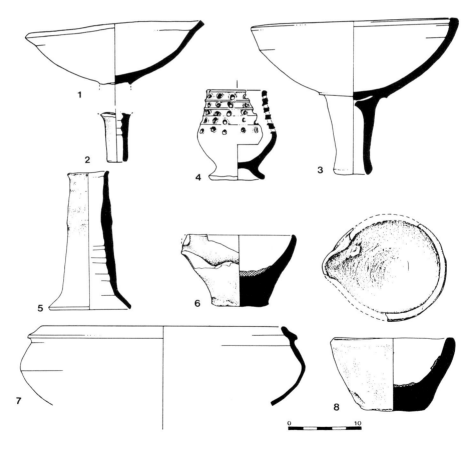

117.   Pottery vessels from Stratum IVB: 1–3 — chalices; 4 — incense cup; 5 — stand;
       7 — cooking pot; 6, 8 — crucibles

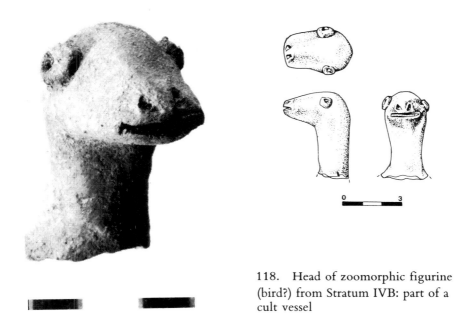

118. Head of zoomorphic figurine (bird?) from Stratum IVB: part of a cult vessel

of the settlement may have something to do with it being near the entrance to the city in the Israelite period. Smaller workshops must have existed in other parts of the large mound. For example, in Area Y in the northeastern section of the town, a furnace was found containing copper oxide-colored ash, slag, burnt olive pits, a circular stone installation and broken blow-pipes. In Area K, in the southeastern part of the site, slag was found in a clay installation which may have been part of a furnace. These remains are also from the Israelite period and are contemporary with the extensive metal workshops at the city entrance. Until now, no workshops later than the beginning of the 10th century B.C.E. have been found. The decline of the industry may be the result of the establishment of the Israelite monarchy which, with its centralized administration, assumed the monopoly over industrial activities and put an end to local workshops.

CHAPTER X — THE SACRED PRECINCT

It is generally assumed that in antiquity — and in our own day as well, for that matter — wherever large numbers of people gather, a center dedicated to worship is established. Indeed, archaeological excavations often prove this to be correct, even though the nature of such remains is not always clear. Sometimes written or historical documents help in the identification of a temple temenos, a high place, an altar, a sanctuary or cult center. At Tel Dan a cult place or religious center from the days of the Israelite monarchy — and from the days of the Danites — presumably exists somewhere

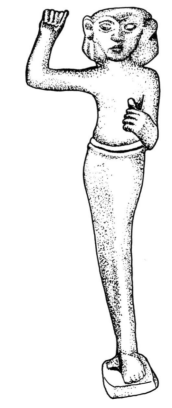

0   3

119. Bronze figurine of female warrior (goddess?) in smiting pose (see also Pl. 24)

120. Egyptian statuette found in a secondary use context in a Late Israelite wall

within the mound. This assumption is based on two explicit biblical texts: "And the children of Dan set up the graven image..." (Judges 18:30) — in the days of the conquest of Laish, and "...he set the one in Beth-el and the other [golden calf] put he in Dan. And...the people went to worship... even unto Dan" (1 Kings 12:29–30) — at the time of Jeroboam I. However, the texts neither describe the physical and architectural character of these ancient cult places, nor do they give an indication of their precise location.

When we started the rescue excavation in 1966, we knew that a figurine belonging to a group called in archaeologists' parlance "Female Warriors in Smiting Pose" had turned up a few years earlier on the banks of the spring, at the foot of the western slope of the mound. The figurine, a goddess with an Egyptian-style wig, is tentatively dated to the second half of the 2nd millennium B.C.E. Could this be an indication that there was a sanctuary nearby?

Several years later, when excavating in Area T near the spring, two Egyptian fragments of a cultic nature were uncovered. The first, found in secondary use among the stones of an Israelite wall of the 9th century B.C.E., is a statuette of red granite depicting a person sitting cross-legged and wearing a long dress, and with the position of the hands suggestive of prayer. According to the study of B. Brandel and A. Ophel, it belongs to a group of statuettes of the personal or private category that was common in the Egyptian Middle Kingdom and in the 18th dynasty, in the first quarter of the 2nd millennium B.C.E. The inscription on the statuette mentions the name of the owner, the priest Nefertem and that of his father, Seti. Although the name Seti as a personal name appears earlier, it is more common in the New Kingdom, especially the 18th and 19th dynasties. Thus, our statuette may well date from the 14th century B.C.E. The second Egyptian fragment was found by chance on the surface of the mound in 1982. According to A.B. Schulman it belongs to a type known as "block-statue." The statuette mentions the god Amun and originally could have been a block statue of the 2nd millennium B.C.E., possibly from the 12th dynasty. However, it was reused and reinscribed later, in the second quarter of the 1st millennium B.C.E.

The discovery of Egyptian statuettes at Tel Dan is not surprising. Egyptian incursions over the land-bridge to Mesopotamia, and at times even domination over this territory, is a central theme in the ancient history of the Fertile Crescent. Whether these statuettes, which are cultic in nature, represent an Egyptian sanctuary at Tel Dan cannot be established. But it may be of some significance that they were both found in the vicinity of the Dan springs.

121. Area T in the early stages of excavation

The area around the springs, one of the three sources of the Jordan River, at the northern part of the site, attracted our attention from the outset. Here was an abundant fresh-water source. Mount Hermon towered above, to the west was the Lebanon mountain range, and the fertile plain of the Hula Valley with its rich, dark basaltic soil extended all around the site. It was a likely place for a king to build his palace, a priest to erect his temple, a scribe to preserve his archives. Exploring this part of the mound, we were intrigued by a large, flat plastered surface with linear grooves that appeared to represent the remains of a wall and a doorway. In 1968, when we began the excavations of this area, henceforth known as Area T, we seemed to be headed for disappointment. The plastered floor looked as though made of modern concrete and at least one of our supervisors insisted that this floor was a recent construction of the Israel Defence Forces, and pointed out that the commanding officer had established his headquarters nearby and his tents had been set up on this platform.

Nevertheless, we decided to persist in our efforts. At the western end of the plastered floor, we uncovered a semicircular construction not unlike the apses commonly found in ancient Byzantine churches. Its orientation toward the east seemed to confirm that we had come across a church. However, we soon realized that we had in effect uncovered a lime-kiln of recent date that had been dug into a massive, ancient stone construction. We proceeded to excavate this almost square construction that was built of well-dressed limestone ashlars laid in header and stretcher fashion, i.e., alternate long and short sides facing outward. This technique is a hallmark of the public buildings dating to the Israelite monarchy uncovered in such places

122. Area T after several seasons of excavation

123. Header-and-stretcher construction at the southern side of the high place

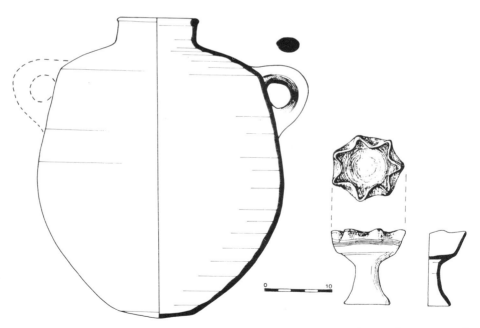

124. Storage jar and one of the seven-spout oil-lamps uncovered at the beginning of
      the excavation in Area T (see also Pl. 25)

as Jerusalem, Samaria and Hazor. When later in the season we found an
Astarte figurine near the southern corner of the structure, and a storage jar
together with several seven-wick oil-lamps west of it, we were reasonably
sure that we had found a cult center.

The discovery in 1974 of a four-horned altar confirmed our impression
of the cultic nature of Area T in the northern part of the city. Because of
the expanse of the platform which covered most of the square structure,
we referred to it at the time as a bamah (high place) — perhaps an open-air
sanctuary. As the excavation area was extended, it became clear that the
structure was part of a large complex which constituted the sacred precinct
or sanctuary of Dan throughout nearly to a millennium and a half.

The Time of Jeroboam I

The earliest evidence of a cultic character found in the course of the excavation goes back only to the 10th century B.C.E., to the time of King
Jeroboam I, the son of Nebat. It was he who, following the death of Solomon, established the northern kingdom of Israel and set up a golden calf
at Bethel and one at Dan in order to prevent the people from going to the
Temple in Jerusalem and thereby swearing allegiance to the Davidic
dynasty. Dan and Bethel were chosen because they were cities at the northern and southern borders of Jeroboam's kingdom. But there was yet
another reason for this choice. The establishment of new cult centers in
these two cities emphasized the continuity of a long religious tradition. In
Bethel that tradition reached back to the days of the patriarch Jacob, and
at Dan to the very first settlement of the tribe of Dan. Conceivably, the
Danite sanctuary or its remains still existed in the days of Jeroboam — or,
at least, the people may still have remembered the religious center originally established by their forefathers. It is therefore likely that Jeroboam
I deliberately set up the golden calf in the original Danite sanctuary. That
earliest sanctuary has not been discovered; future excavations may reveal
evidence of cultic practice dating to that period beneath the existing massive stone structures.

The earliest remains in Area T which may be interpreted as cultic were
uncovered under a thick layer of crushed travertine. Walls built of large
basalt and dolomite fieldstones and boulders, two complete pithoi with a
snake decoration, an incense stand, the broken fragments of a clay tub with
a shelf used as a seat, and other vessels led us to conclude that we were digging within the sacred precinct of the city of Dan of the 10th and beginning of the 9th centuries B.C.E. The date, based on the ceramic evidence,
corresponds with the time of Jeroboam I's reign. We did not find the

125.   The "snake" pithos with two pottery vessels *in situ*

126.   The "snake" pithos after restoration

127.   Seal impression on the rim of one of the "snake" pithoi (see Fig, 128:1)

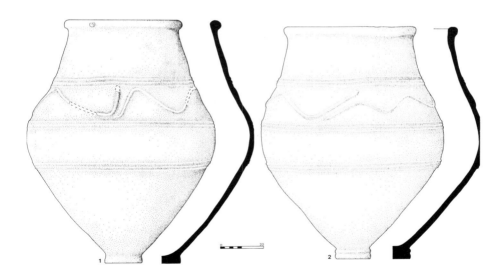

128.   Two pithoi decorated with snakes in relief

golden calf. Its precious gold was no doubt carried off by any one of the foreign kings who conquered Dan. But even without the golden calf the excavations uncovered enough evidence to enable us to reconstruct King Jeroboam I's sanctuary at Dan.

The sacred precinct at this time occupied about 60 x 45 m. Encompassing the precinct were rooms and open areas. More than 45 m. of the western line of the precinct have been exposed. In one of the sections we found a sunken amphora filled with ashes and surrounded by a ring of stones. At the north end of the same section was a small sunken installation consisting of five upright stones. Exposure of the eastern side was much more limited and we only know now that the precinct extended beyond the excavated area there. Remains of a massive structure built of large, dressed travertine blocks were uncovered in the northern part of the precinct. The southern face of this structure has been exposed along 18 m. When it was first discovered, we thought of it as being a high place, or bamah. Since it seemed to be the earliest, we called it Bamah A. In view of the extensive remains of that period discovered subsequently, it should be considered part of Stage A of the sacred precinct erected here by Jeroboam I. South of the structure is a 28 x 17 m. complex which included a central building, roofed storerooms, an open cobbled courtyard, a sunken basin with two basalt slabs on either side, and a pool installation.

At the northern end of the central complex were three storerooms. Truly spectacular finds were discovered in a 5 x 2 m. cell — two upright pithoi, jugs painted in red and black stripes, red-slipped bowls, and an amphora stand. The pithoi, each of over 300 liter capacity, were decorated with an encircling snake relief. On the rim of one pithos was a seal impression of a male figure with each of its outstretched arms grasping the horns of a rearing ibex. Next to the room where the pithoi were found was another storage room with a large quantity of broken vessels. By counting the identifiable parts, and reconstructing the assemblage, we reached the figure of 40 vessels, mostly storage jars of medium size, among them an unusual Phoenician juglet. Phoenician influence is also evident in the shallow bowls or plates found next to the pithoi and other vessels. That the vessels and objects bear an affinity to Phoenician material culture is not surprising. The close commercial and cultural relations between Hiram of Tyre and Solomon no doubt continued, and probably intensified, under Jeroboam I and the kings of Israel who ruled after him — as may be understood from the marriage of Ahab and Jezebel. The rooms excavated here had been destroyed by a fire that swept through the complex, burying the rooms and their contents below the collapsed mud-brick superstructures.

At the heart of the central complex, is a ca. 7.5 x 5 m. construction of

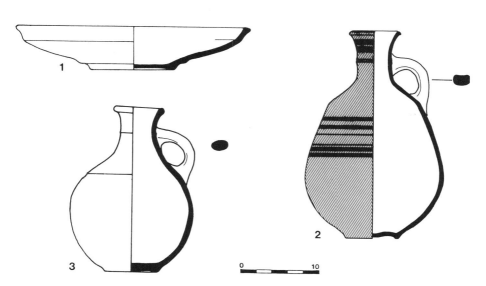

129. Pottery vessels found with the "snake" pithos: 1 — bowl; 2, 3 — jugs

130.   Storeroom with broken vessels on the floor

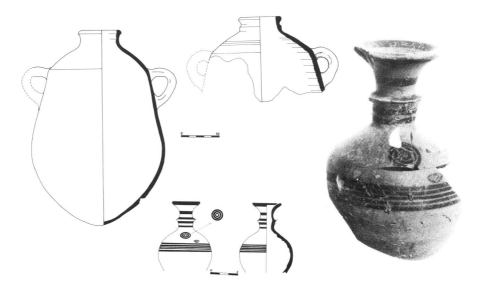

131.   Storage jars and a Cypro-Phoenician juglet from the floor of the storeroom

132.   Pebble floor where the incense stand was found

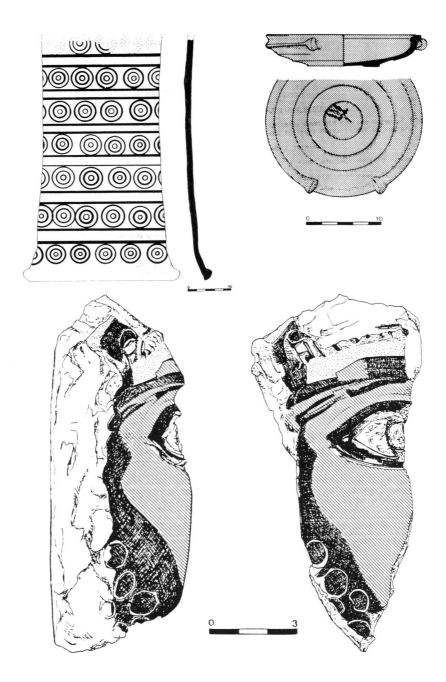

133.   Incense stand; a bar-handle bowl with a trident incised on the base; and the head
        of a male figurine found on the pebble floor (see also Pls. 26–28)

basalt boulders partially covered by two layers of immense travertine blocks — probably the foundation of a structure which originally rose higher. The entire superstructure and a large part of the central section of the foundation were robbed of their stones already in antiquity. A cobbled courtyard originally surrounded the structure. The cobbling was found along the southern face of the preserved blocks where it extends 4.5 m. southward, reaching the northern wall of the basin installation described below. The cobbled pavement was also found in the east, 2 m. beyond the travertine block structure, and it extends to the east wall of the central complex. On the cobbles lay a decorated incense stand, the head of a male figurine, and a bar-handle bowl full of small animal bones and with a trident incised on its base. Since no signs of burning, collapsed brick or roofing were found here, the cobbling appears to have been part of an open-air interior courtyard in the middle of which may have stood the central altar.

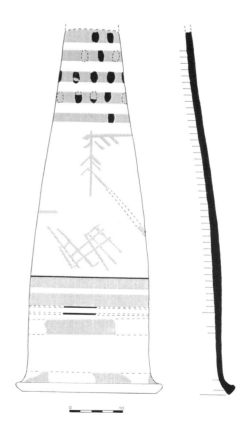

134. An additional, restored incense stand

135.   The stone-lined basin and the incense stand found in one of its walls

A remarkable feature at the southern end of this complex is the spring pool. Originally this appears to have been a simple oval-shaped basin surrounded by flagstones, separate from the complex. Some time later, the west wall of the complex was extended southward and a pool was built east of the wall. The pool included the eastern portion of the original installation. A new wall built to the south of the pool enclosed it on that side. Two steps led into the 1.5 x 1 m. rectangular pool. On the stone pavement leading northward the fragments of a large terra cotta tub were found next to the wall. When the tub, which presumably served some cultic purpose, was restored it was found to be 1.41 m. long, 82 cm. wide and 65 cm. deep. It is now exhibited in the Skirball Museum of Biblical Archaeology in Jerusalem.

The discovery of a sunken basin and flanking basalt slabs north of the spring installation and the tub aroused much speculation. Built into a raised terrace of pebbles and bricks along the west wall of the complex was a symmetrical building: in the center was a basin (1.4 × 0.88 m.) flanked by

136.   Sherds of tub *in situ*, and the restored tub

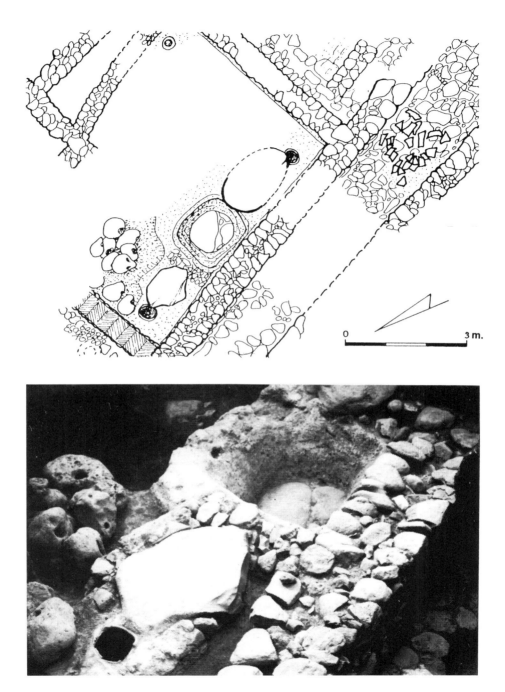

0   3 m.

137.   Plastered basin with basalt slabs at both ends

two very large, sloping basalt slabs leading to two large sunken jars. The southern slab had a groove cut into the tip where it met the jar. A group of twelve dolomite boulders of different sizes and weights were found to the east of the basin. Each stone has what seems to be a naturally-formed hole at one end. Three of the stones weighed 25, 40 and 70 kg., respectively. The floor sloped to the south and east, down to the rim of a large sunken basalt receptacle in the southeast corner of the area.

The jar at the southern extremity of the installation contained a shallow bowl and a faience head of an Egyptian king wearing the white crown of Osiris. In the jar at the end of the northern basalt slab was a fragmentary faience figurine of a monkey seated beside the lower part of a person, perhaps a king or deity. Also in this jar was a fragment of a male clay figurine similar to the one found on the cobbled floor next to the decorated incense stand described above. Another faience figurine, which may represent the torso of an Egyptian deity or king holding a staff or lotus stem, was found near the broken fragments of a pithos with a snake decoration. This was the third pithos with a winding snake motif discovered at Dan. It was found about 15 m. south of the first two, immediately north of the basin installation. It may be of some significance that of the many pithoi uncovered in the course of our excavations at Tel Dan, pithoi with snake decorations were found only in the sanctuary area. The snake figures prominently in the Bible during the wanderings of the Israelites in the desert of Sinai (cf. Numbers 21:9). A bronze snake was kept in the Temple of Jerusalem for many centuries, until the days of King Hezekiah (2 Kings 18:4). Pithoi with snake decorations have been found elsewhere, notably in the sanctuary of Enkomi in Cyprus, but these are of an earlier date.

What was the function of the plastered installation? At first sight it seemed to be part of an oil-press. But this idea was dismissed: the bottom of the basin, which was not plastered, would allow valuable olive oil to seep through. The complete absence of olive pits, and the tremendous quantity of gray ash and burnt bone fragments in and around the basin, suggested some sort of animal sacrifice. The large stones lying around the installation may have served as tethers or weights. However, the lack of drainage provisions precluded any activity involving large quantities of blood. The most logical explanation is that the liquid in question must have been water — readily available and ritually significant. In this connection we recalled the pottery tub discovered on the stone pavement leading to the rectangular pool whose water level is the same as that of the spring about 15 m. away. These installations may have served in water libation ceremonies antedating the drawing of water festivities during the Second Temple Period. According to the Talmudic literature, these festivities originated very early

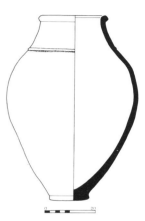

138.   Storage jar found at the southern edge of the basalt slab.

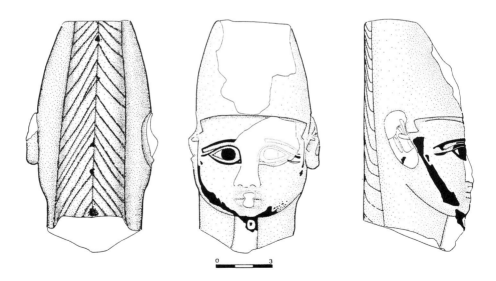

139.   Head of a faience figurine of an Egyptian king wearing the white crown of
       Osiris found inside the above storage jar (see also Pl. 31)

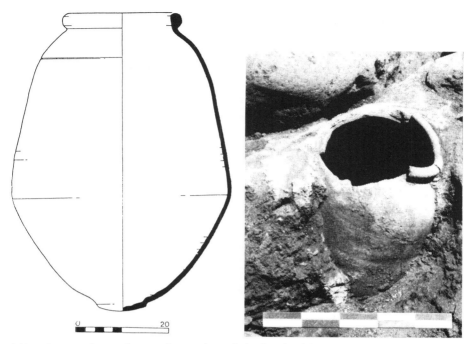

140. Storage jar at the northern edge of the basalt slab

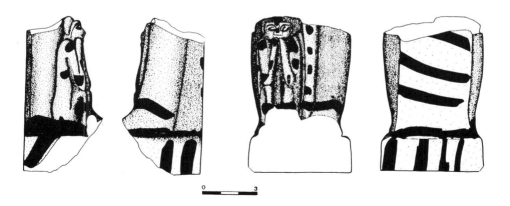

141. Faience figurine of a monkey sitting at the foot of a person or deity found in the above storage jar (see also Pl. 30)

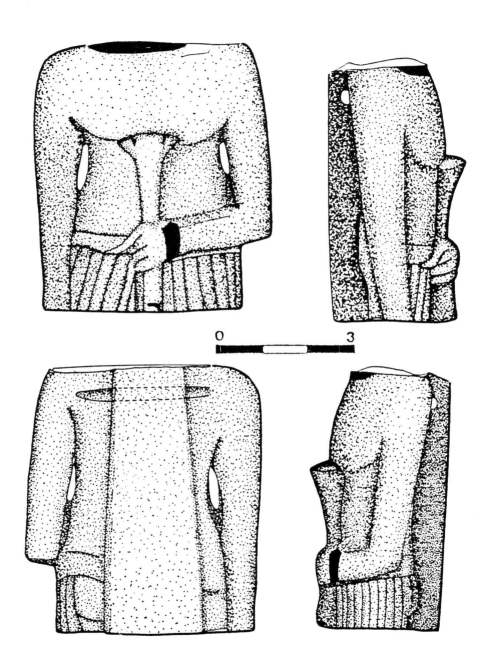

142.   Faience figurine of an Egyptian king or deity holding a lotus stem, found north
        of the jar in Fig. 140 (see also Pl. 29)

in the history of Israel. It was said to be a rite that went back to the days of the prophets, or with Moses on Mount Sinai, indicating that the exact origin was unknown but that the tradition was ancient. Two such occasions are recorded. One was on the eve of the war with the Philistines, when the people gathered at Mizpeh and "drew water, and poured it out before the Lord" (1 Samuel 7:6), and the second when David refused to drink the water brought to him from the well in Bethlehem and instead offered it as a libation to God — "poured it out unto the Lord" (2 Samuel 23:16). Water also plays a major role in Elijah's consecration of the altar on Mount Carmel, and water is mentioned in Ezekiel's prophecies relating to the Temple (Ezekiel 47). It seems that the archaeological excavations at Tel Dan have now uncovered installations connected with water libation ceremonies from the end of the 10th-beginning of the 9th centuries B.C.E.

The remains uncovered in Area T and dated to the end of the 10th-beginning of the 9th centuries B.C.E. belong to the structures erected by Jeroboam I when he set up the golden calf at Dan. Whether a temple was also built or whether these are the remains of an open-air sanctuary is difficult to say. As to the religious practices at the site, we can only refer again to 1 Kings 12:27–31 which states that Jeroboam I was concerned lest the people go to Jerusalem to "offer sacrifices" and provided them with an alternative venue for sacred rituals at Dan. Jeroboam appointed priests — but not from the tribe of Levi. Since Bethel is mentioned in connection with the priests of the bamoth (high places), we can infer that this also applied to Dan. At Bethel, Jeroboam I celebrated a new feast and "offered [incense] upon the altar" (1 Kings 12:33). Presumably he did so at Dan as well. The sanctuary of Dan may have superseded that of Bethel. The statement in 1 Kings 12:30 that "the people went [or followed]...even unto Dan" seems to suggest the primacy of the golden calf sanctuary at Dan. Where was the golden calf set up? Very likely, it was placed on one of the platforms or in one of the buildings uncovered within the area of the sacred precinct. Perhaps all the remains found in the sacred precinct are of the "house of high places" which Jeroboam "made" (1 Kings 12:31). These are the most extensive late 10th-early 9th century B.C.E. cultic remains so far uncovered in Israel.

How long did the sanctuary built by Jeroboam I at Dan remain in use? Probably not more than a generation or two. Evidence of fire on the red burnt stones of the northern platform — the one referred to as Bamah A, and a layer of ash found inside the store rooms attest to the destruction of the sanctuary complex. Additional evidence is to be seen in the wanton destruction and intentional scattering of ceremonial cult objects throughout the entire excavated area. This may have been wrought by the army

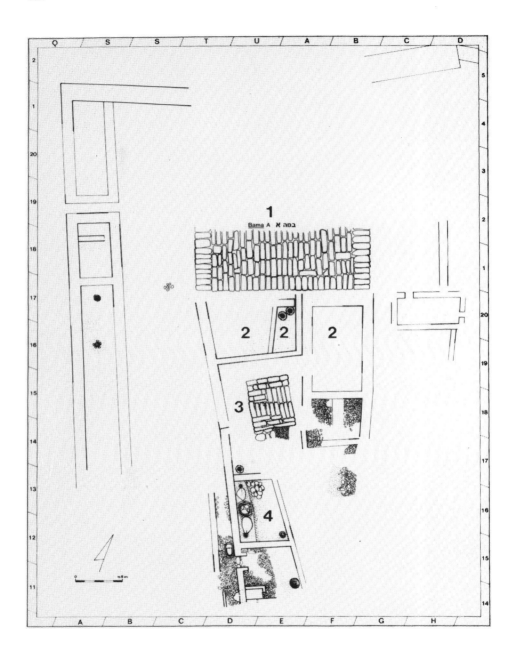

Bama A במה א

143.   Plan of the sacred precinct in the days of Jeroboam I: 1 — bamah; 2 — storage
rooms; 3 — podium of altar; 4 — the plastered basin (see Fig. 137)

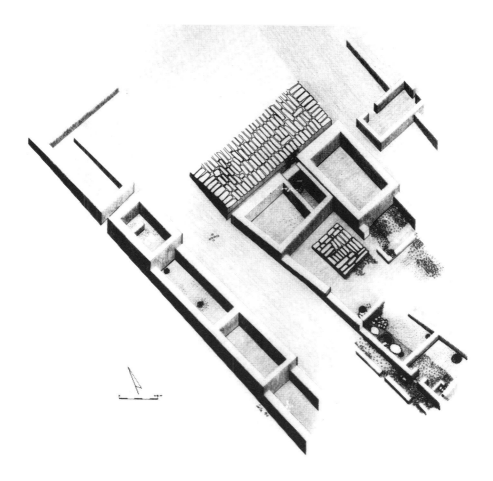

144.   Reconstruction of the sacred precinct from the time of Jeroboam I

of King Ben-hadad of Damascus. Following the deaths of Jeroboam I in
Israel and Rehoboam in Judah, conflict sharpened in the divided monarchy
over disputed areas in the southern part of the northern kingdom. The bal-
ance of power shifted in favor of Israel during the reign of Baasha. In his
distress, King Asa of Judah turned to Ben-hadad, king of Aram-Damascus
for help. Ben-hadad invaded Israel and Dan was among the cities he
"smote" (1 Kings 15:16 ff.). The biblical narrator's choice of this word is
significant, for apparently the city of Dan (our Stratum IV) was not visited
by total destruction.

The Time of Ahab

The sacred precinct at Dan smitten by Ben-hadad did not remain desolate for long. The discovery of the thick travertine floor encompassing the massive, square stone structure marks a new conceptual and architectural stage in the development of the sacred precinct. During this phase (Stratum III), the massive, almost square structure built of ashlars, referred to as Bamah B was erected. The construction is surrounded in the east, west and south by a 10–20 cm.-thick surface, consisting of crushed yellow travertine, that we called the "yellow floor." This yellow floor was laid over the remains of the earlier sanctuary enclosure, with the exception of the central block structure, and extends over a large area. It slopes downward along the original steep incline of the Middle Bronze Age. The impressive ashlar construction, the central block structure, and the yellow floor now become the dominant and identifying features of the sacred precinct — not only in this phase of its existence but for generations to come.

Although not completely preserved, the dimensions of the ashlar construction of Bamah B are probably the same today as when originally built: north face 18.03 m., east face 18.63 m., south face 18.39 m., and west face 18.82 m.; northeast-southwest diagonal 26.1 m., and northwest-southeast diagonal 26.05 m. On three sides the structure is built of finely dressed ashlars laid in header-and-stretcher fashion. On the northern side, only the corners are built of ashlars and the rest of the walls are of rough basalt boulders. This made good economic sense since that side was not seen by the public. Where it was revealed, the width of the ashlar construction is 1–2 m. The stones are dressed in the classical technique common to Israelite royal buildings of the 9th–8th centuries B.C.E. The enclosure is bisected by an east-west basalt wall 1.9 m. thick. Two north-south walls, also 1.9 m. thick, bond with this wall and with the northern wall of the structure, and divide its northern half into three compartments. The southern half is built of fieldstones, but these were laid in orderly fashion, course upon course, testifying to the importance of the structure.

An interesting feature of the ashlar construction is the step, 3–12 cm. high and 20 cm. wide, cut into the lower course along the entire length of the eastern face of Bamah B, and found also along sections of the southern and western faces. This step is seen also at the northwest corner of the structure. We noted that wherever preserved, the stones of the course above the stepped one were found in a down-slanting position. It seems that originally wooden beams were integrated into the ashlar construction, and when the wood rotted away the stones above it either collapsed or remained in a slanting position. We recalled in this connection that Solo-

145.   The southern side of High Place B with the "yellow floor" at the bottom which
        covers remains of the preceding phase

mon "built the inner court [of the house of the Lord] with three courses
of hewn stone and one course of cedar beams" (1 Kings 6:36; 7:12), and
that King Cyrus of Persia decreed that the Temple of Jerusalem be similarly
built "With three rows of great stones and a row of new timber" (Ezra 6:4).

146.   Part of the eastern side of High Place B; the "yellow floor" is at the left

147.   Tilted stones and the stepped recess in the eastern wall of the high place (top center)

The discovery of a stepped recess cut lengthwise along one of the ashlar courses confirmed our assumption that wooden beams were integrated in the construction. These were held in place by means of rectangular dowels whose slots are visible in the recess. The slots, 10 cm. long and 3 cm. deep, are located at irregular intervals and were also found in the stones of the structure's bisecting wall and on several stones in secondary use. The slots and the step feature are seen also in the northwest corner of Bamah B, indicating that originally the building rose much higher.

One of the problems the builders had to contend with was how to create a horizontal surface on the slope of the Middle Bronze Age rampart. To this end they used basalt boulders as a foundation and laid the travertine ashlars on top. This mode of construction can be seen on the eastern and western sides of the structure. On the southern side, the existing travertine block structure of Bamah A provided a sound foundation and here the entire wall is built of ashlars. In some places this wall is preserved to a height of 1.4 m. above the yellow floor, but it must have been at least 1.25 m. higher — if indeed it was built to the height of the preserved northern side.

148.   The stepped recess in one of the ashlar courses for insertion of wooden beam in the wall; note the rectangular dowel slots

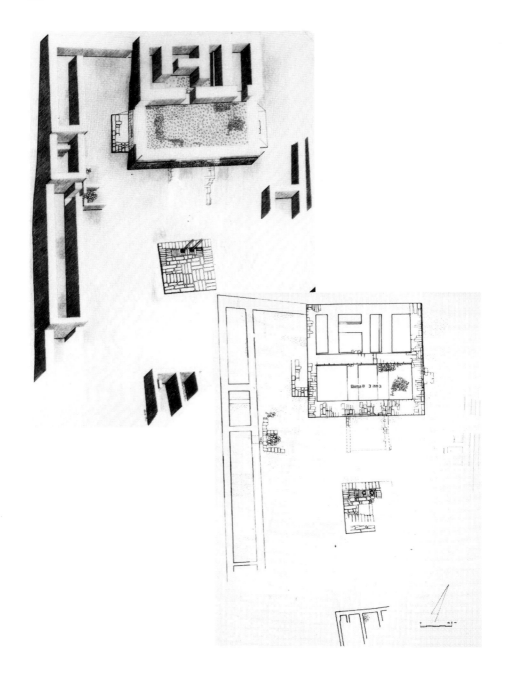

149.   Plan and reconstruction of the sacred precinct from the time of King Ahab

When we first uncovered the massive structure of Bamah B we were impressed by its remarkable size. For the people coming to the sanctuary, especially from the south, the ashlar construction rising at least 3 m. above the well-built courtyard must have been an imposing sight. Such was the bamah where Samuel officiated: "...there is a sacrifice of the people to day in the high place" (1 Samuel 9:12–14,19); from which the prophets descended (1 Samuel 10:5); and the "high place" which Solomon "built... for Chemosh" (1 Kings 11:7). Who built Bamah B and its surrounding courtyard, and when? The dating derived from the pottery collected on the surface of the yellow floor could tell us nothing since later construction had removed the earlier remains and swept the floor clean in places. The pottery found beneath the yellow floor provides the latest possible dating. As this pottery is from the first half of the 9th century B.C.E., the construction of Bamah B with its yellow floor must have occurred around the mid–9th century — roughly 860–850 B.C.E. This was the time of Ahab's reign, the king who fortified Dan and built the gate complex and city wall at the southern side of the town. Ahab had the means, and apparently the inclination, to restore also the sanctuary at Dan to its former glory — and even beyond it. If so, it was he who built the monumental ashlar construction (our Bamah B) with the impressive yellow-floored courtyard around it. Whether Ahab also introduced the worship of Baal at Dan, as he did in Samaria at the instigation of his Phoenician wife Jezebel, we cannot know. The famous encounter between Elijah and the priests of Baal took place on Mount Carmel. The only mention of Dan in the Ahab account is a general reference to his following the sinful ways of Jeroboam the son of Nebat (1 Kings 16:31).

How did the people get to the top of the impressive Bamah B structure? We do not know the answer. On the east and west side of the structure we did find remains of a flat area built of stone slabs abutting the yellow floor. These slabs may perhaps suggest that steps or a ramp existed here when the structure was in use. This question still awaits further investigation.

Other changes within the sacred precinct of Dan were also undertaken when this ashlar structure was built. Some 12 m. south of the bamah a pavement of travertine slabs was added along the northern side of the dressed travertine block construction that remained from Stage A of the sanctuary precinct — the time of Jeroboam I. This addition extends 2 m. beyond the original structure to the east. The new travertine pavement has the same orientation as Bamah B. On the pavement, near and parallel to the northern edge, are two plastered circles, 50 cm. in diameter and 1 m. apart. The circles most probably mark the position of two columns that

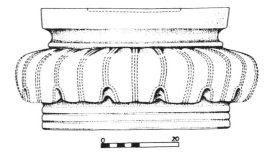

150. One of the two plastered, circular spots marking the place of column bases; the
      drawing below is of the column base found elsewhere in secondary usage, which
      matches the spot

were not found. Perhaps the base of a column in secondary use, built into a late Hellenistic wall, may have come from here; the diameter of this base is the same as that of the circles. The midpoint between the two columns lines up exactly with the center of the bamah's south face. This planned symmetry is striking. As the midpoint between the two circles is 4 m. from the western edge of the pavement, the original width of the pavement was probably 8 m. Its preserved north-south length is 7 m. At the southern end of the sacred precinct, above the pool installations of the previous period, a new building was constructed, of which only the western part has been exposed.

The Time of Jeroboam II

The family of Ahab was annihilated in the second half of the 9th century B.C.E. The subsequent reigns of Jehu and Jehoahaz were a time of political and economic decline for the kingdom of Israel. The precarious security situation along the northern border of Israel most probably also affected the status of Dan as a religious center. From an archaeological aspect, this situation is reflected in the lack of new construction of that period. However the decline did not last long. The Assyrian threat from the North forced the Arameans to desist from fighting Israel, and King Jehoash, Jehu's grandson, laid the foundations for a renewed, more powerful kingdom of Israel. At the beginning of the 8th century B.C.E. the Arameans were defeated and expelled from the regions of the country they had conquered. The accession to the throne of Jeroboam II, the son of Jehoash, in 785 B.C.E. ushered in a period of expansion and prosperity. Jeroboam II conquered Damascus in the east and "restored the coasts of Israel" as far north as "from the entering of Hamath..." (2 Kings 14:25). The city of Dan benefitted greatly from this and the cultic precinct underwent appreciable development.

The grandeur of the sanctuary in the days of Ahab and Jeroboam II can now be better appreciated as a result of the restoration work being carried out by the Antiquities Authority on behalf of the Israel Government Tourist Corporation. The robbed courses of ashlar header-and-stretcher construction have been replaced to reach the highest point of preservation, and today the south face of Bamah B rises 3 m. above the surrounding courtyard. Along the east face of the bamah a wooden beam has been set into the stepped course where originally there must have been a cedar beam, as mentioned above. The sloping stones uncovered in the course of the excavation have been reset over the wooden beams and an additional course has been restored above these. During our excavation we had removed nearly half of the steps of the monumental staircase leading to the bamah from the south that were built by Jeroboam II. These steps have now been replaced. And the small probe down to Bamah A, just east of the steps, has been enlarged so that the construction of Bamah A can now be followed to the southeast corner of Bamah B.

"In which direction should the excavation be extended?" is perhaps the most frustrating question for the expedition director seeking additional information to what has been uncovered so far. While everything the archaeologist's spade brings forth is of interest, one can never escape apprehension at missing something important in the unexcavated areas. When we decided to open the area west of the Bamah B structure, we kept wondering about what might be hidden beneath the path we trod daily, on the east side of the bamah, and whether we should have focussed our efforts on that direction instead. As it turned out, our choice was a good one, and the discoveries made west and south of the bamah have given us new insights into the activities of the sacred precinct in the 8th and following centuries B.C.E.

About 15 m. southwest of the bamah, a room 7.25 x 4 m. with walls 80 cm. wide (Room 2844) was uncovered 1.5 m. below the surface of the mound. Entrance to the room was both from the east and the west. On the floor we found a square construction measuring 1.03 x 1.03 m. and 27 cm. high made up of five uneven limestone blocks with a round, flat stone on top. The stones are soft and porous with traces of fire on the surface. This construction clearly postdates the yellow floor. When it was first discovered we tried to guess its function. Was it the base of a pillar supporting the roof or the base for an altar — or even the altar itself? The discovery of a bronze bowl about 1.5 m. east of the structure was suggestive but not conclusive. However, when two iron shovels were found 70 cm. north of the structure, and a third 1.05 m. to the south, we knew that we indeed had an altar. The discovery of the upper half of a jar sunk upside-down in the ground and full of ashes, some 20 cm. south of the structure, absolutely confirmed this identification. The three shovels found around the altar were each made from one piece of iron. The two that were found together are 54 cm. long with scoops 14–15 cm. long, about 11 cm. wide and 2–5 mm. thick; the handles are about 1 cm. thick. Both have hooks and rings at the end of the handles, probably for hanging on a wall. The third shovel is somewhat longer, 57 cm., and may have been longer still as the end of the handle is missing. The scoop is elongated and is 16 cm. long and 11 cm. wide. Thus, two of our shovels are approximately one biblical cubit long, and although the Bible does not give us the dimensions of these cultic utensils we felt justified in using the biblical term *maḥtah* and *ya'eh*, translated

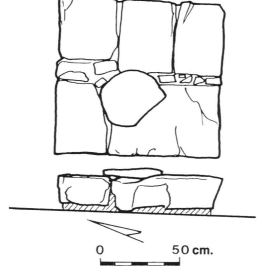

151.   Altar built of five stones

as censers, for our shovels. Such shovels are also represented, albeit with shorter handles, in the mosaics of synagogues of the Roman and Byzantine periods.

The altar is about 2 cubits across and half a cubit high; its dimensions

152.   Two of the three iron shovels found near the altar (see also Pl. 33)

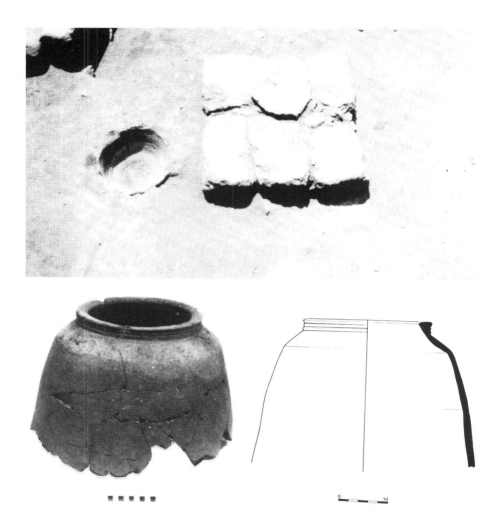

153.   The altar and jar containing ashes *in situ*; below — the jar after restoration

suggested that it was an incense altar. The preliminary analysis of the ashes found in the sunken jar by Neutron Activation Trace Element tests shows that they include burnt bones. The same results were obtained from the ashes of the second jar excavated under the yellow floor in the altar room and dated to an earlier period. The iron shovels were apparently used to remove the ashes from the altar to the jars. Therefore the altar may have served also for animal sacrifice. The animal bones found in the excavated areas are being examined by the anthropologists P. Wapnish and B. Hesse of the University of Alabama at Birmingham. The results of their tests will

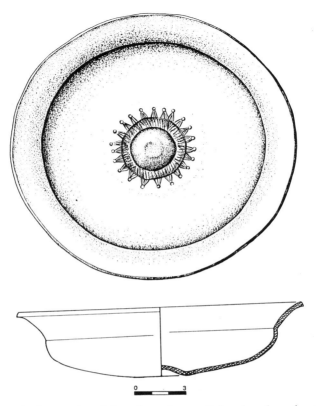

154.   The bronze bowl found southeast of the altar (see also Pl. 34)

throw light on the intriguing problem of sacrifice in the sacred precinct
in general, and in the altar room in particular. Additional confirmation for
Room 2844 being an altar room came at the end of the 1986 excavation
season, when two additional altars built of travertine were found next to
the southern wall of the room. The larger of these altars is 44 cm. high
and has a slightly concave top. The corners flare outward about 19–22 cm.
The smaller altar is 30 cm. high and in its top surface is a squarish, recessed
hollow measuring 23 x 21 cm. Both altars show traces of fire.

The exquisite carinated bronze bowl found in Room 2844 has an
omphalos base and is 16 cm. in diameter and 5 cm. deep. The exterior is
badly corroded, but on the inside the lotus leaf decoration is preserved.
Bowls of this type were used extensively in the ancient Near East.
Assurbanipal and his queen are seen holding cups of this type while feasting

155. The altars at the southern end of the altar-room

in their garden. King Yehawmilk of Byblos presents a libation to his goddess in a similar bowl. Since the bowl was found in the altar room we presume that it was used for cultic purposes.

When we removed the stones of the altar for exhibition in the Skirball Museum in Jerusalem, the head of a scepter was discovered on the floor below. Made of bronze and hollow in the center, it is 9 cm. high and 3.7 cm. wide. Four badly corroded figures, possibly representing lion heads, jut out from the top of the artifact. Below the figures, three circular grooves form four veins, or rings, a motif that appears three more times on the scepter head. The middle section consists of a protruding bronze ring with silver leaves, and the base is a protruding flange. The discovery of the scepter head caused much excitement, for here was the head or top of a scepter similar to those held by kings and priests — and in at least one case, by a goddess. Symbols of authority, scepter heads have been found in a number of excavations. They appear often in ancient texts and Egyptian art. In the Bible, the only mention of a scepter is that which King

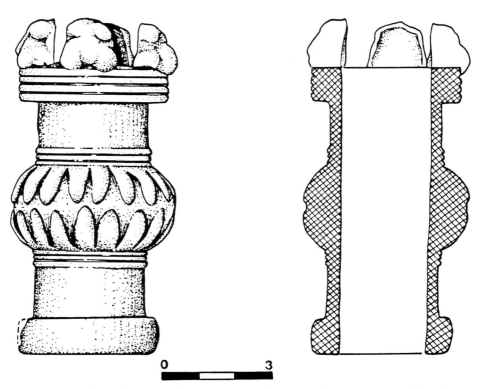

156. Head of the bronze and silver scepter found under the stones of the altar (see also Pl. 32)

Ahasuerus extended for Queen Esther to touch (Esther 5:2). However, that scepter was of gold and the story of Purim is dated some 400 years after the time of Jeroboam II. A number of similar scepter heads were found at Nimrud in Mesopotamia.

The altar room was part of a larger complex along the western enclosure wall of the sanctuary, of which other rooms were excavated. South of the altar room was a 7.5 m.-long room entered from the courtyard on the east. Two flat basalt stones, 2.5 m. apart, were found with a 2 m.-long burnt wooden beam lying on the floor, one end resting on the southernmost stone. On the northern stone were remains of charred burnt wood. The conclusion was inevitable — two wooden posts stood on the stones. North of the altar room was a small annex reached through a doorway 90 cm. wide, with an ashlar sill. Here we found a die made of blue faience or frit which may have served the priests in divination. The spots indicating the numbers are inlaid in white and every two opposing facets add up to the number seven.

North of the annex room, outside the enclosure wall, the excavation revealed a room (No. 9024) of special interest. Only the eastern part of the room was excavated and inside we found an amphora handle stamped with the name "ImmadiYo." Room 9024 is located approximately 15 m. north of the altar room and, although it is at a higher level, belongs to the same period (Stratum II). *ImmadiYo* means "God is with me." It brings to mind the name Immanu-el (Emmanuel) meaning "God is with us." The

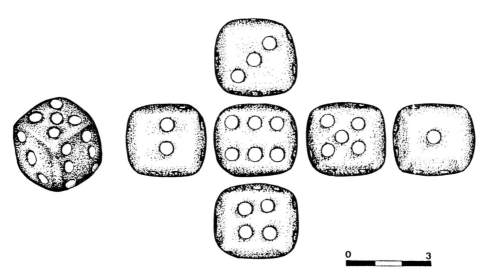

157.   Faience die for prognostication or gambling (see also Pl. 37)

0   1

158.   Seal impression of ImmadiYo

theophoric ending *Yo* is the same as *Yahu* in Judah. Indeed, the name Immadi-Yahu has recently been discovered in Judah on an ostracon in Horvat ʿUza in the Negev. There it appears in conjunction with his father's name — "Immadi-Yahu the son of Zakar." In our excavations, the discovery of the stamped handle with the name ImmadiYo enabled us to decipher another such handle discovered at Dan in 1974 which we did not succeed in reading at the time. By comparing the two and observing the similarity of some of the letters, we concluded that this jar handle also belonged to a person called ImmadiYo. We cannot be sure that the House of ImmadiYo served a cultic purpose, but the fact that it adjoined the wall of the sanctuary raises such a possibility. Perhaps ImmadiYo was an officiating functionary at the sanctuary.

The stamped amphora handle with the name ImmadiYo was found in a thick layer of destruction that contained several broken vessels, some of which were restored. The pottery and epigraphic analysis of the ImmadiYo date the stamped handle to the 8th century B.C.E. ImmadiYo thus lived at the time Jeroboam II embarked on a massive building program in the sanctuary area. Among the undertakings of Jeroboam II were the construction of a magnificent central altar, the ashlar wall surrounding it, and the monumental staircase on the southern side of the bamah.

159.   The stairway built during the reign of Jeroboam II

160. Stepped construction at the southwestern corner of the central temenos

161. Horn of a large altar found in the debris near the steps

The staircase leading up to the bamah is 8 m. wide, and the side walls are constructed of ashlars. It is built against the south face of Bamah B, over the yellow floor. The excavation revealed an earlier, 6.2 m.-wide, staircase of indeterminate date built on top of the yellow floor, also leading up to the center of the bamah's southern face. The monumental staircase starts 3.75 m. from the bamah. Assuming that the stairs reached the top of the bamah, the highest step would have been 2 m. above the present preservation level of this structure. The bamah of this period must have been an impressive structure — in keeping with the centrality of the cult at Dan. Not less impressive were the new central altar and the enclosure wall of ashlars measuring 14 x 12.5 m., with entrances on the east and south. These entrances are 1.6 m. wide, their door jambs protruding into the courtyard. In the southwest corner of the ashlar enclosure were five steps, each 1.5 m. long and 50 cm. high, and three steps in the northeast corner. These steps led to the top of the structure, probably the central altar of the sacred precinct in the 8th century B.C.E. On removing the baulk from a previously excavated square we found a large, horn-shaped stone, 50 cm. high and a base diameter of 39 cm., which may have been part of an altar. A horn of similar dimensions was found in Megiddo. We can only conjecture the size of an altar with such horns. If we are right in assuming that the proportion of the horn to the height of the altar is about 1:6, the altar would have been 3 m., or 6 royal cubits, high.

Built into the northwest corner of the ashlar enclosure wall is a 1.4 x 1 m. stone installation with its own flagstone pavement. Approximately 30 cm. south of this installation we found a four-horned limestone altar with a heavily calcined upper surface. The dimensions of the altar are 38 x 40 x 35 cm. On such an altar small burnt offerings were made, and evidence of the fire that consumed them was still visibly embedded in the surface. It is doubtful that the altar was found where it had originally stood. This discovery, in 1974, further emphasized the cultic importance of the area under excavation and confirmed our view as to the centrality of the cult at Dan. It was with good reason that the prophet Amos castigated the people who swear by the god of Dan. The prophet, in his wrath, foresaw the calamity that befell the nation: "They that swear by the sin of Samaria, and say, Thy god, O Dan, liveth...even they shall fall, and never rise up again" (Amos 8:14).

God's instrument for punishing the people of Israel was Assyria. In 733–32 B.C.E. Tiglath Pileser III, king of Assyria, invaded the northern kingdom and conquered Ijon, Abel-beth-maachah and Hazor. Dan is not mentioned either in this passage of 2 Kings 15:29 or in the annals of the Assyrian king. However, in our excavations we encountered a layer of

162.   Four-horned altar

destruction by fire dated by archaeological evidence to the second half of
the 8th century B.C.E. ImmadiYo's house, the altar room, the annex and
the pillar room were all destroyed by this conflagration.

A similar fate befell another building nearby, where such a thick layer
of destruction was also uncovered. South and slightly west of the sanctuary
precinct, near the spring, a thick layer of destruction was discovered by
chance in the excavations of 1987 while removing excavation material
dumped there in previous seasons. A gaping hole appeared, at the bottom
of which was a water channel. Although we traced parts of the channel
during the 1988 and 1989 seasons, we could not determine whether it
served to convey water from the spring or whether it was a drainage channel under the floor of the building. The channel is built of stone and roofed
with stone slabs.

The function of this building (No. 9235) could not be ascertained even
after three seasons of excavation. It must have been of considerable size,
at least 25 x 10 m., with a well-laid flagstone pavement and stone walls
separating the rooms and courtyard area. The destruction of this building
had been fierce. The walls collapsed and the mud-bricks were burnt red;

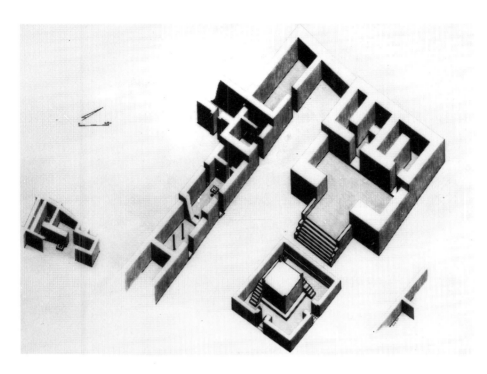

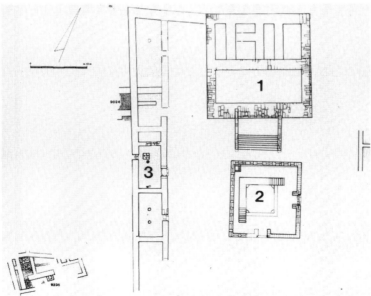

163. Plan and reconstruction of the sacred precinct in the days of Jeroboam II:
      1 — bamah; 2 — altar; 3 — altar room

164.   Conflagration level dated to the Assyrian conquest

the debris was over 1 m. high in some places. A large number of vessels
were found in the destruction. Among these were storage jars, jugs, kraters,
cooking pots, a basalt bowl and a figurine in the form of an ox which may
have been part of a ritual vessel known as a kernos — consisting of a hollow
ring with a several little animal-shaped receptacles on it. This building, at
the edge of the sacred precinct, may have served the needs of the officiating
priests or devotees. It was destroyed at the time of the Assyrian conquest,
as was the house of ImmadiYo and the altar room. This destruction marks
the end of Stratum II at Dan.

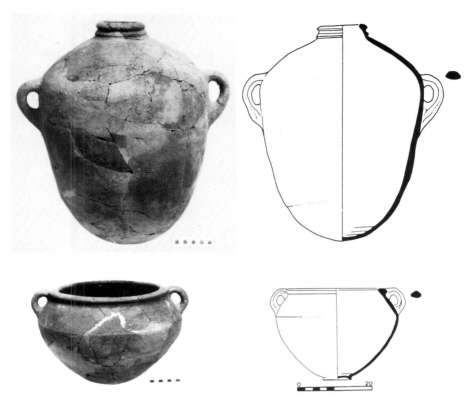

165. Storage jar and krater found in the conflagration level of the House of ImmadiYo

166. Vessels found in the Assyrian conflagration level

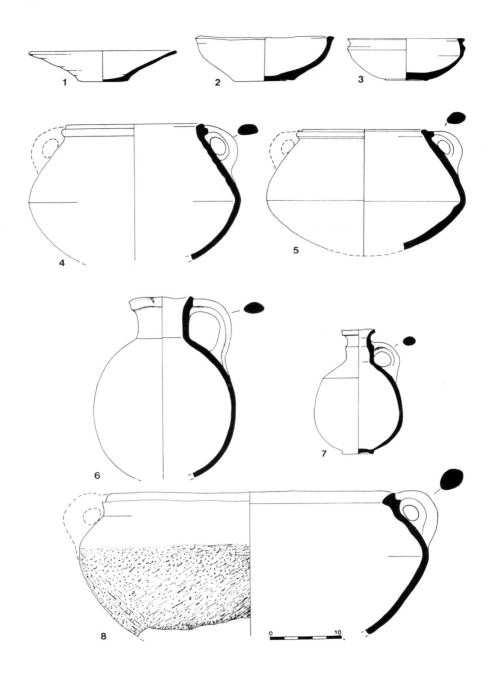

167. Pottery vessels dated to the second half of the 8th century B.C.E. found in the
      conflagration level: 1–3 — bowls; 4, 5, 8 — cooking pots; 6 — jug;
      7 — decanter

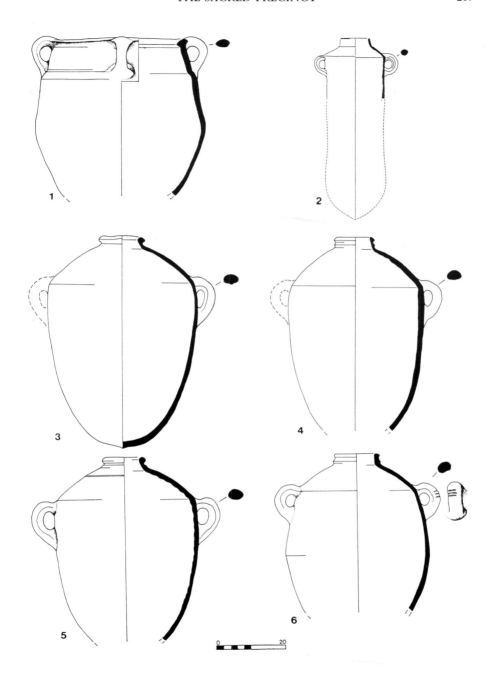

168. Additional pottery vessels, second half of the 8th century B.C.E. from the
      conflagration level: 1 — krater; 2–6 — amphoras

169.   Water channel, remains of Building 9235, and Wall 8703/8810 above them

After the Assyrian Conquest

We can only speculate as to what happened at the sacred precinct immediately following the Assyrian conquest. The Bible tells us that the descendants of Moses's grandson "were priests to the tribe of Dan until the day of the captivity of the land" (Judges 18:30), which occurred at the time of the Assyrian conquest in 733–732 B.C.E. The Assyrians implemented a policy of exchanging the native population with people from distant lands. Whether the priests of Dan also went into exile, and whether one or more of them returned, as was the case in Bethel (2 Kings 17:24–28) we are not told. In any case, our findings showed that the sacred precinct at Dan continued to function.

In the 1984 season a rectangular building (No. 2746), measuring 19.7 x 6.5 m., was excavated in the northwest corner of the sacred precinct. The foundation trench for the eastern wall is clearly visible where it cuts the yellow floor. Six pilasters about 80 cm. wide and projecting about 25 cm. from the wall, are spaced 2–2.5 m. apart. They were probably intended as an architectural enhancement of the western wall. Two 40 cm. -high, plastered tables or benches were built along the east and south walls

170. Building 2746 that perhaps served as priestly chambers, 7th century B.C.E.:
     1 — north entrance; 2 — east entrance; 3 — the tables

171. Two benches, or tables, in the south part of Building 2746

172. Faience figurine in Egyptian-Phoenician style from Building 2746 (see also
      Pl. 36)

of the structure at its southern end. There were two entrances: in the north
an 1.2 m.-wide ashlar doorway led to a sloping pavement also built of
ashlars; and in the east, another 1.2 m.-wide entrance had a doorsill built
of flat stones inclined inward toward the floor level.

Along the southern wall of Building 2746 was the wall of another building (No. 2770). The easternmost of this partially preserved structure had
a thick yellow floor, while the area immediately to the west, built over the
burnt remains of the ImmadiYo house, had a light-blue plaster floor. A
plastered opening in this floor led to a 1 m.-long drain meticulously carved
from a single dressed travertine block and capped with a second carved
stone. The drain stone was sunk into the south wall of the destroyed building. Small stones set at the base of the drain stone may mark the southern
continuation of the channel which was apparently removed later. It may
be that Building 2746 served as a *lishkah* or chamber connected with the
sanctuary complex. The Bible mentions chambers that King Hezekiah prepared in the house of the Lord (2 Chronicles 31:11), and others are referred

to in Jeremiah 35:4. Whether these were similar to the one at Dan we cannot say. According to the Bible, tithes and offerings were brought to these chambers. Nehemiah, for example, "cleaned the chambers...and thither brought...the vessels of the house of God, with the meat offering and the frankincense" (Nehemiah 13:9). In earlier days Samuel took Saul and his servant to a chamber and ordered the cook to serve them a meal (1 Samuel 9:22–25).

At some stage, the south wall of Building 2746 was breached and the walls of Building 2770 were removed; the *lishkah* was enlarged towards the south. At that time or perhaps somewhat later, a wall was built across the northern end of the *lishkah*, the northern ramp was covered and the eastern entrance was narrowed by the addition of a new ashlar doorjamb. A faience figurine of Egypto-Phoenician style was found under a gravel floor. The building continued in use during the 7th century B.C.E., as did the other rooms along the western wall of the enclosure, although their function at this time is not clear. In the altar room a new doorsill and floor were laid over the altar and a poorly-preserved installation was built against the west wall of the room. To the south of the altar room we found a room with ashlars standing along the north, west and east walls — to what purpose, we do not know. Remains of six engaged pilasters, each 1.1 m. wide

173.   Wall 8703/8810 with pilasters built after the Assyrian conquest

and spaced 2 m. apart were uncovered along more than 17 m. south of the
northwest corner of the room.

Southwest of the cultic precinct, on the destruction level of Building
9235 described above, were found the remains of an imposing public building (No. 9214). Of its northern wall (Wall 8703/8810) 25 m. have been
cleared, but it extends also further to the east and west. Its eastern courses
were laid on the stones of the earlier wall. In the north face of this wall
are seven, possibly eight, engaged pilasters. The pilasters, spaced about
1.5 m. apart, are 1.3–1.5 m. long and 50 cm. wide. The wall and the pilasters were badly damaged, and only one of them was preserved to a height
of 1.4 m. The building was destroyed at the end of the 8th or beginning
of the 7th century B.C.E. Among the vessels found in destruction layer of
Building 9214 were storage jars, an almost complete bowl and two stone
rollers for compacting and levelling floors or roofs. It was probably a public
building, perhaps the Assyrian governor's. Soon after the destruction of the
building the character of this area changed, and during the 7th century
B.C.E. it became domestic in nature.

In the Persian Period

The political and military instability following the Babylonian and Persian
conquests, no doubt also had an impact on the cultic activities of the sacred
precinct at Dan. A few architectural remains uncovered on the west side
of the sanctuary attest to its continued use, although in the southern section, one building apparently functioned only until the end of the Persian
period. In the courtyard of this building two Macedonian coins of the 4th
century B.C.E. were found. A number of small cult objects were uncovered, including a terra cotta figurine of the god Bes represented as a
paunchy, bow-legged dwarf. The god Bes, a favorite among the people,
protected women in childbirth, mothers and children. His cult was wide-
spread in Egypt, Cyprus and the Phoenician coast. The figurine of Bes from
Dan exhibits a mixture of Egyptian and Phoenician stylistic influences.
Among the other figurines was that of a woman carrying a child, a horse
and rider, a Horus temple boy, two bronze representations of Osiris, two
bronze bracelets with an animal representation (a calf?) on one of them,
and the head of a goddess of the Persian period — the 4th century B.C.E.
Although these objects and other fragments were found in a temple reposi-
tory (favissa), not much more can be said at this time about the activities
at the sacred precinct during the Persian period — except that it continued
to exist.

0   3

174. Figurine of the god Bes of the 4th–3rd centuries B.C.E. (see also Pl. 38)

In the Hellenistic Period

Numerous remains of the Hellenistic period enable us to conclude that the
sacred precinct at Dan continued as a major cultic sanctuary throughout
the 3rd and 2nd centuries B.C.E. and must have attracted many pilgrims
and worshipers. At least two phases could be distinguished in the Hellenistic period. The entire temenos now changed its orientation and was encom-
passed with narrow walls built of fieldstones laid in herringbone fashion,
and an entrance in the south. The west side of the temenos is not parallel
to the bamah structure but faces it slantwise, toward the north.

   In the first stage of the Hellenistic period a large building, with at least
six rooms, was erected in the western part. The eastern wall of this building
extends to the northwestern corner of the existing ashlar building (originally, Bamah B) and passes over it. The western wall continues for 45 m.
from north to south, and bonds into an ashlar-built corner with the southern wall. A Hellenistic juglet found between the stones of the lowest course
of this wall gave us the definitive date of the wall. The southern wall was

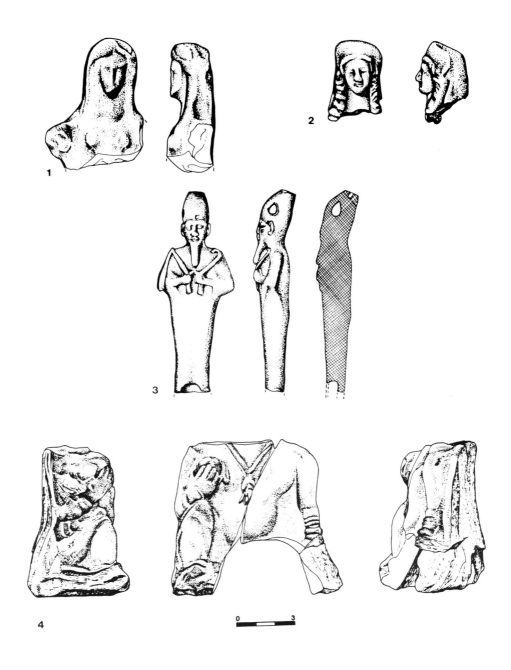

175. Figurines of the 5th and 4th centuries B.C.E.: 1 — woman with child; 2 — female head; 3 — Osiris, in bronze; 4 — temple boy (see also Pls. 39, 40)

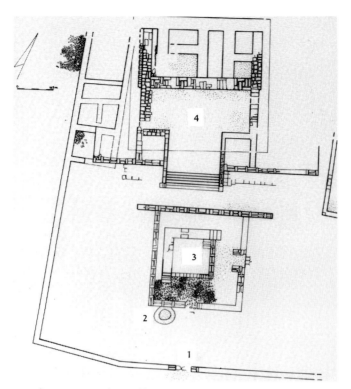

176. The sacred precinct in the Hellenistic period: 1 — entrance; 2 — water reservoir; 3 — place of altar; 4 — stone pavement

177. The entryway in the southern wall of the Hellenistic precinct blocked in the Roman period

178.   Coin of Ptolemy II, left — obverse; right — reverse

uncovered eastward along 38 m., and must have extended at least 5 m. more. The entrance, built of ashlars, is 2 m. wide. Two architectural components of basalt, originating from earlier Israelite structures, appear as building material in the southern wall. One is a tapering Egyptian obelisk-type pillar, and the other the column base we mentioned in connection with the construction of Ahab's time. The stones of the walls are laid in herringbone pattern with ashlar-built corners and have been preserved to a height of 1.3 m. Another building, also with herringbone walls and ashlar corners was found east of the bamah with an ashlar-built entrance in the west wall. Outside the entrance a 3rd century B.C.E. oil-lamp was uncovered.

Additional courses of stone were laid on the original bisecting east-west wall of the bamah structure. Presumably, on the northern half of the original structure a building was erected — possibly a temple. We were unable to identify these remains because much of the late construction was in a poor state of preservation. The approach to the new complex was by the monumental staircase from the days of Jeroboam II at the south. Also continuing in use were the 8th century B.C.E. ashlar enclosure walls and stairs in the central part of the temenos. Twelve coins of Ptolemy II (284–247 B.C.E.) found in the course of the excavation date the period, and there were local and imported wares. Most of the local vessels were made of yellowish-brown clay with red-brown slip decoration. Especially common were tall, pear-shaped juglets with full-disk bases, wide shoulders and mushroom-shaped mouths. There were cooking pots of red-brown clay, their rims and shoulders trimmed in a careless manner in red-brown slip.

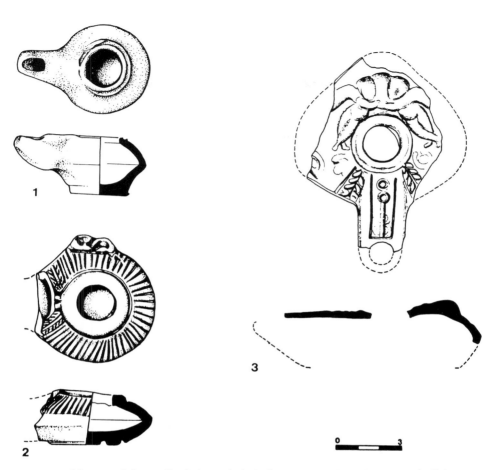

179. Oil-lamps of the Hellenistic period, 2nd century B.C.E.: 1 — round oil-lamp;
2 — with incisions pattern; 3 — with relief of two winged boys

The oil-lamps are mold-cast, with high rounded bodies, an elongated nozzle and full base. Among the imported vessels fish-plates with a shallow
depression in the center and everted, elongated rims and ring bases were
common, as were thin-walled semi-globular bowls. One large Megaran
bowl decorated with a vegetal motif in relief was found.

In the 2nd century B.C.E. imported, mold-cast oil-lamps painted with
red-brown slip were common. The usual type is a rounded lamp with a
broad filling-hole, a ridged pattern on the shoulder and a carinated handle
on the side. Among the oil-lamps was a lyre-shaped one decorated with
two embracing cupids in high relief, and with an elongated nozzle. Assemblages of this kind, combining locally-made and imported wares, are

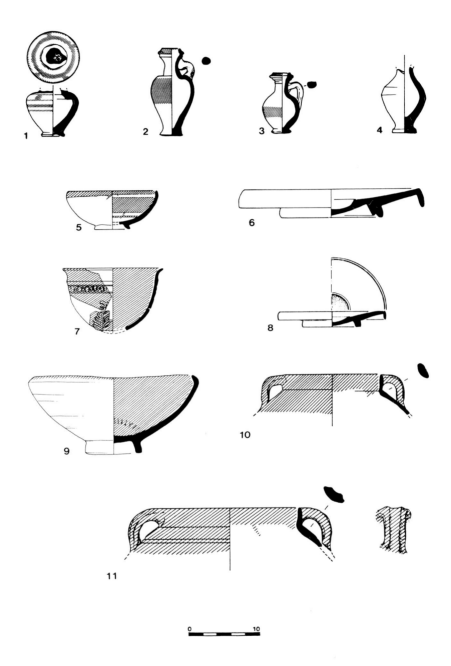

180. Pottery vessels of the Hellenistic period, 3rd–2nd centuries B.C.E.:
      1–4 — juglets; 5, 7, 9 — bowls with red slip; 6, 8 — "fish-plates;"
      10, 11 — cooking pots

common in sites of the period and recall in particular the vessels of the Hellenistic period from Tel Anafa, not far from Dan, near Kibbutz Shamir.

Two important discoveries dated to the Hellenistic period were made in the course of the excavations and belong either to the first or second Hellenistic phase. The first discovery was of a sunken, cylindrical plastered basin attached to the southern outside face of the ashlar enclosure wall. Plastered on the outside and inside it appears to be a water basin having a diameter of 1.5 m., 1.1 m. high, and walls 60 cm. thick. Getting into it was facilitated by a toe-hold on its eastern side. The basin may have served for some ceremony connected with divination. It was a common practice in the Hellenistic world to seek the oracle by throwing an object into a water basin. No water conduit was found; the water was probably brought to the basin from the spring in various vessels. When a part of the basin collapsed, we found in the debris fragments of crenelated limestone blocks dated to earlier periods — perhaps from the original entrance to the central ashlar enclosure of the Israelite period.

But the peak of excitement came in 1976 with the discovery, north of the Hellenistic basin, of a bilingual Greek and Aramaic inscription incised in stone. It is always thrilling to find an inscription — they are so rare — but to find one mentioning the name "Dan" and "its god" was extraordinary! Moreover, any doubts as to the identity of the city we were excavating were now definitively laid to rest. The inscription — obviously not *in situ* — was found lying face down, some 17 m. south of the 9th-century-B.C.E. ashlar building, beneath a floor of the Hellenistic period. The inscription is cut into a flat limestone slab, 25.6 cm. long, 18.2 cm. wide and 3.2 cm. thick. The edges of the slab are damaged, and criss-crossing lines were incised in it. The inscription is in three lines in Greek and one line in Aramaic. The form of the Greek letters points to the Hellenistic period, the 3rd–2nd century B.C.E.; the Aramaic letters are of the same period. The inscription may be dated to the first half of the 2nd century B.C.E.

The Greek text is quite clear, although the first letters in Line 2 and in Line 3 are damaged. It tells of a person named Zoilos (Zilas, in Aramaic) who made a vow "to the god who is in Dan." Zoilos is a common name in Greek onomastics of the 4th–2nd centuries B.C.E. One Zoilos who was the tyrant of Straton's Tower (Caesarea) of the 2nd century B.C.E. is mentioned by Josephus Flavius. The Aramaic part of the inscription is more difficult to decipher since a few letters are missing at the beginning and end of the line. However the word *ndr* is clear. Before this word is the upper part of a letter, probably a terminal *nun*. There is room for two more letters which could have been *bet* and *dalet*. If so, the first word in the Aramaic line would read *bdn*, i.e., "in Dan." At the end of the line there is room

181.   Plastered basin of the Hellenistic period

■ ■ ■ ■ ■

ΘΕΩΙ

ΤΩΙΕΝΔΑΝΟΙΣ

ΙΩΙΛΟΣΕΥΧΗΝ

TO THE GOD

WHO IS IN DAN

(VOWED) [Z]OILOS A VOW

[V]OW ZILOS TO THE G[OD]

182.   Bilingual Greek and Aramaic inscription: "To the god who is in Dan"

for three letters after the letters *lamed* and *aleph* — possibly, *lamed*, *heh* and
aleph. Thus the suggested reading of the word would be *lᵓlh'a*, meaning
"to the god." The whole line in Aramaic would then read "In Dan Zilas
made a vow to the god" — which is the Aramaic version of the Greek.

Thus, from the inscription we know of Zoilos or Zilas, of Dan, and of
a vow. The hard questions are: who is the god of Dan (or in Dan), and
is there any significance to the word Dan in Greek appearing in the plural
form? The god of Dan is not mentioned by name. If Zoilos had a Greek
deity in mind, he would have called on the god by his name, as is customary
in Greek inscriptions. It seems to us that Zoilos made his vow to a deity
so well known at Dan that its name need not be mentioned. Many centuries
before Zoilos, the prophet Amos, when referring to the popular oath "Thy
god, O Dan," also does not mention the name of the deity. The reference
to the locality in the Greek plural form need not be of special significance.
This is not uncommon in Greek sources, and if our reading of the Aramaic
text is correct, it would support the view that the word "Danois" refers to
the site. If however, the term "Danois" refers to the people living in the
town, it would mean that they considered themselves to be the descendants
of the tribe of Dan.

During the second Hellenistic phase, building activities seem to have
centered around the northern ashlar structure. It was extended 5 m. to the
east, 4 m. to the west and 2 m. to the south, using the ashlar blocks of previous buildings. A 32 x 22.5 m. surface with an imposing 32 m.-long southern facade was thus created. The monumental staircase was now partially
recessed into the new surface, and rooms were built flanking both sides of
the recessed steps. On both sides of the steps and along the facade, a beautiful ashlar slab pavement covering five of the original steps was built. The
pavement formed a wide and impressive avenue in front of the enlarged
structure with perhaps a shrine or temple built on it. This second phase of
the Hellenistic period may be attributed to the time of the Seleucid dynasty.
Coins from the days of Antiochus III (223–187 B.C.E.) to Demetrius II
(146–140 B.C.E.) were found. To this period also dates the statue of Aphrodite discovered by chance in a field near the site. Though we cannot be
sure, it is a fair assumption that it came originally from Dan.

A large number of 2nd century B.C.E. amphora handles bearing Greek
names were found in a concentration of broken vessels just to the west of
the sanctuary. Other imported vessels of the period included fish plates,
black slip ware and oil-lamps. With this assemblage were large, thin-
walled amphoras, made locally by hand. These vessels, found also in other
parts of the sacred precinct, belong to a newly-identified pottery group of
this period from the Golan Heights and have been attributed to a local tribe

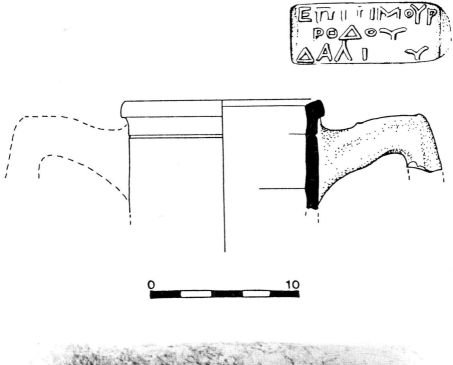

183. Seal impression on a Rhodian jar handle, 2nd century B.C.E., with eponym
      "Timoyr" = Timur; the month Dalios in the inscription corresponds to
      September-October

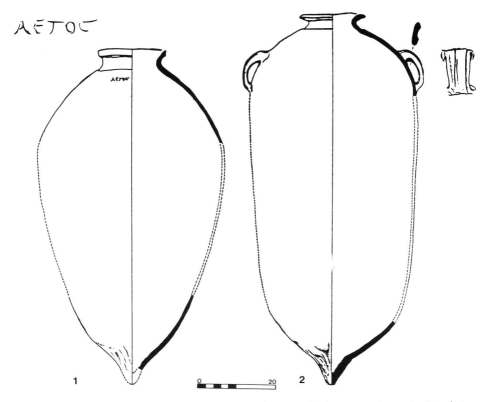

184.   Storage jars of the 2nd century B.C.E. (Iturean?); the name Aetos in Greek is
       incised on the shoulder of the jar on the left

or people known as Itureans. The amphoras are large vessels made by hand
of coarse red-brown clay. They have long barrel or sack-like bodies. The
everted rims are turned on a wheel and attached to the neck of the vessel.
Usually potters' fingerprints can be seen on the wide handles. We know
almost nothing of the Itureans who are named after one of the sons of
Ishmael (cf. Genesis 25:5 and 1 Chronicles 1:31). According to Josephus
Flavius, the Hasmonean King Aristobolus conquered part of their country
and forced them to accept Judaism. The classical sources relate that the
Itureans inhabited also the slopes of Mount Hermon and the land of
Bashan, and parts of Lebanon. The personal names of Iturean soldiers men-
tioned in Roman inscriptions are mainly Aramaic.

185. Juglet of the 4th–3rd centuries B.C.E.

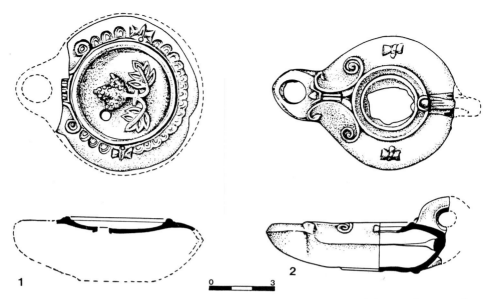

186.   Roman oil-lamps, 1st –2nd centuries C.E.: 1 — closed disk-type lamp with
       relief of grape cluster and leaves; 2 — with volutes and double-axe motif
       (see also Pl. 41)

In the Roman Period

Considerable changes took place in the sanctuary precinct during the
Roman period. Here too, at least two phases can be distinguished. At the
beginning of this period the stairs to the bamah structure continued in use,
with the addition of at least three steps at the top. A new travertine floor
surface was laid over the southern half of the original ashlar structure. A
wall was then built against the southern Hellenistic temenos wall, blocking
the entrance. The floor level of the sanctuary area was raised, and the new
Roman floors were laid on top of the Hellenistic remains. To the west, the
new Roman temenos wall was outside the Hellenistic temenos and parallel
to the bamah structure, reverting back to its original orientation in the Israelite period. In the center of the Roman temenos a wider enclosure of fieldstones was built over the earlier ashlar one. But the entrances remained
from the east and south.

The monumental staircase and sumptuous facade eventually fell into dis-
use. Huge travertine blocks were piled over the steps and along the facade,
covering both, and travertine blocks were set along the east face of the original structure. The bisecting wall on top of the ashlar construction was

187.   Pottery fragments of the Hellenistic period *in situ*

replaced by a new one along its south face, and new walls were erected at the northern half of the structure. An almost complete cooking pot of the 3rd century C.E. was found on a well preserved travertine floor. A new and even thicker floor of crushed travertine was laid over the southern half of the structure. The original orientation of the sanctuary seems to have changed now to east-west. Among the finds of the beginning of the 2nd century C.E. were two disk-type oil-lamps. These were mold-cast and covered with a red-brown slip. Especially common is the spiral relief pattern flanking the rounded nozzle. One of the oil-lamps is decorated with a cluster of grapes in high relief. Around the shoulder is a chain of circles with two small double-axe devices.

An elaborate system of water installations was exposed in the course of the excavation near the spring. Terra cotta pipes conveyed water from the spring to outlying areas. About 40 m. north of the spring was the fountain house, dug into layers of earlier occupation — a rectangular structure measuring 3.5 x 2.5 m. and built of dressed travertine stones in secondary use. On one of the stones are the Greek letters ΠΑΡ. On the south side of this structure stands a stone wall built of five courses, and next to it, six steps, each 1.3 m. long and 30 cm. high. At the bottom is a surface of flat stones.

At the northern end of the fountain house we discovered a plastered pool, 1.8 x 1.15 m. with a plastered, 7 cm.-deep channel next to it. The pool is divided into two parts by a stone partition wall across which a small channel, 6 cm. wide and 10 cm. deep, is carved to allow the water in both parts of the pool to equalize at that level. The floor of the pool consists of four complete rectangular rooftiles and two incomplete ones. The tiles are incised with X marks. Beneath the tiles a layer of plaster was found laid over stones and broken pottery, and under this is a layer of beaten earth. A terra cotta pipe whose opening was found in the upper, eastern rim of the pool fed the pool with water from the spring. The water outlet is a clay pipe leading to a stone channel 10 cm. wide and 28 cm. deep. The stopper, made of clay, was found *in situ*. The slope of the channel directed the water back toward the spring. Sections of the clay pipe and stone channel were found about 7 m. south of the fountain house where they cut through the pilaster wall of the large 8th century B.C.E. public building. For the water to flow to the pool through the pipe, a dam had to be built to raise the water level at the spring, and remains of a dam built of ashlars in secondary use were indeed found. Only two courses were preserved — 3.5 m.-long in the western wall of the dam and 90 cm.-long in the southern wall.

188.   The fountain house of the Roman period

189. Clay pipe (right center) that conveyed water from the spring to the fountain
      house

When the fountain house was first discovered we thought it might be
a nympheum or a ritual bath, but some of the essential components for
either of these were lacking. We then concluded that our installation was
probably a fountain house, similar to those known in the Roman and Hellenistic world, e.g., in the temple of Apollo at Delphi and the temple of
Asklepios in Corinth. They were built for the use of the public and for cultic ceremonies. At Dan, the fountain house continued the centuries-old tradition of cult at the sacred precinct.

The fountain house was probably built in the early Roman period and
was in use until the 4th century C.E. A number of coins were found around
the fountain house, the latest of which belong to the reign of Emperor
Honorius (394–423 C.E.). The assemblages of vessels from the late Roman
period include numbers of deep, ribbed, large bowls with heavy slanting
walls and rims carinated outward. The pear-shaped stamped oil-lamps are
made of yellowish-brown clay and have flat bases and conical knob handles
with stamped circle patterns on the shoulders. One of the oil-lamps, dated
to the end of the 4th century C.E., marks the end of the sacred precinct
at Dan.

190. Coin of Constantine I (306–337 C.E.) minted in Rome; left — obverse, right — reverse

191. Ornamented oil-lamp of the late Roman period (see Fig. 192:6)

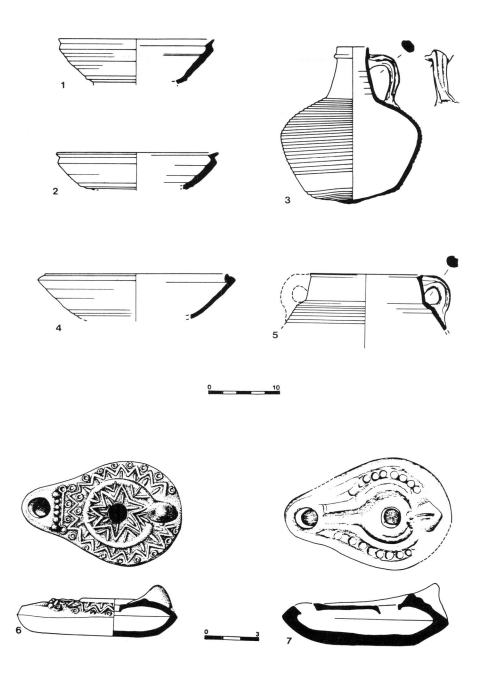

192. Pottery vessels of the late Roman period, 3rd–4th centuries C.E.:
1, 2, 4 — bowls; 3 — jug; 5 — cooking pot; 6, 7 — oil-lamps

CHAPTER XI — THE ISRAELITE FORTIFICATIONS

As often happens in archaeological research, and no doubt in other fields as well, important discoveries are rarely programmed. Indeed, we had no inkling that we were on the track of one of the best preserved Iron Age city wall and gate systems when, during the first two seasons of excavations, part of a wall and a well built stone pavement were uncovered. We suspected that these remains could only belong to some sort of monumental building and referred to them as such. In due course we discovered that the flagstone pavement belonged to one of the largest Israelite gate complexes uncovered in the country.

We had come across the flagstone pavement while investigating the construction of the Middle Bronze Age ramparts. Intrigued by this discovery, we continued the excavation by following the pavement in an easterly direction. Even when we came across what was obviously a stone sill, apparently facing east, we wondered whether it could possibly be an entrance to a public building or even a temple — although entrances to temples usually face west. Only after many seasons of excavations there

193. Threshold and stone with hinge socket (above center) of Israelite city-gate when first discovered; note wear of sillstone (right of center)

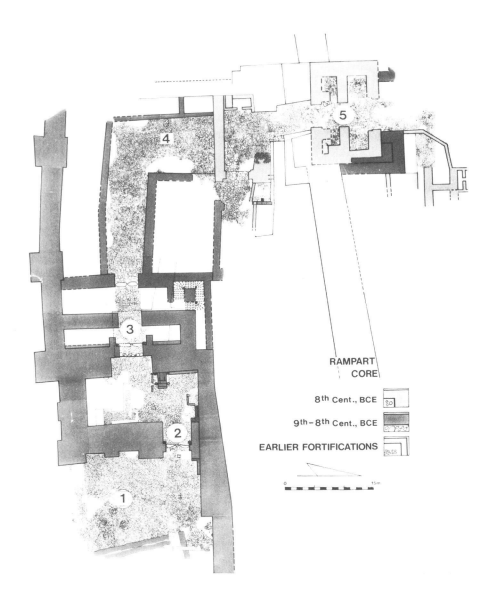

194. Plan of the city-gate of the Israelite period: 1 — the paved piazza; 2 — the outer
      gate; 3 — the main gate; 4 — the paved way; 5 — the upper gate

195. One of the buttresses of the outer, southern wall of the main city-gate structure (Stratum III)

emerged a complete city gate complex in a massive wall. The gate complex consists of an inner main gate and an outer gate; between them, starting from an extensive area paved with large stones at the facade of the outer entrance, a magnificent royal processional way winds to the top of the mound. Three buttresses, each 5 m. long and 12.8 m. from each other, strengthen the main gate's southern outer wall. The buttresses project 1.7 m. outside the line of the city wall and the westernmost one also protrudes 60 cm. inward. Two additional buttresses reinforce the southern wall of the outer gate. Three smaller buttresses on the eastern wall of the outer gate complete the defenses of the gate complex.

The city wall was built at the foot of the mound, partly on bedrock and partly on the lower slope of the earthen ramparts. About 60 m. of the wall's length has now been exposed. It was built of large unworked basalt boulders with a mud-brick superstructure. The stone construction was preserved to a height of 1.4 m. on the west side of the gate complex and an impressive 3.5 m. on the eastern side. Near its northeastern corner we found the wall still coated with the original thick plaster. Among the debris on the pavement were plaster fragments and numerous fallen bricks, some of them still with their plaster coating.

The main gate, consisting of two towers and four guard rooms, measures

29.5 x 17.8 m. The towers measure 4.5 x 3.5 m. each, and the chambers about 3 x 2 m. each. The threshold is 4 m. wide and is made up of large basalt slabs which show considerable wear from the opening and closing of massive wooden doors. The doorstop and one of the hinge sockets have been preserved. From the threshold, the paved roadway paralleling the city wall ascends westward, and after 17 m. turns abruptly to the north, up a 28-degree incline into the city and to the top of the mound.

To the right of the entrance is a bench and a unique structure. The bench, built of ashlars along the outer wall of the northeastern gate-tower, is 4.5 m. long. It was probably on such a bench that the elders of Israel used to sit. When the Psalmist speaks of those "that sit in the gate" (Psalms 69:13) he must have had in mind a bench similar to the one discovered here. A good illustration is given in the Book of Ruth 4:1–2: "Then Boaz went up to the gate and sat down there and behold, the kinsman of whom Boaz had spoken came by; and he said to him...sit down here and he...sat down...and he took ten men of the elders of the city and said 'sit ye down here' and they sat down." Such a bench must also have existed in Sodom: "...and Lot sat in the gate of Sodom" (Genesis 19:1).

Benches at ancient city gates are quite common, but a rectangular structure we uncovered at the southern end of the bench, abutting the eastern wall near the corner of the tower is unique. It measures 2.5 x 1.1 m. and

196.   The city wall at the entrance of the outer gate

197. Base of the canopied structure; note end of stone bench just above right center (see also Pl. 44)

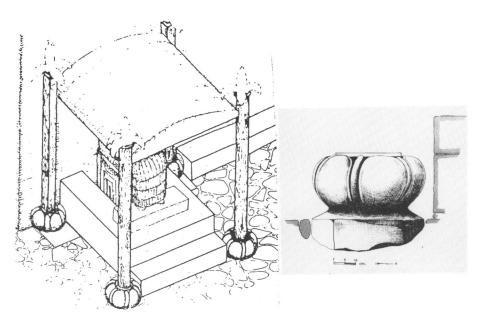

198. Suggested reconstruction of the canopied structure and the monolithic pumpkin-shaped stone

is built of ashlars, with a step in front of it. The two rectangular ashlars, laid at right angles to the tower wall to form a square hollow between them, have opposing rectangular recesses at the inner top edge in their eastern ends — possibly to accommodate another ashlar placed across them that may have served as the base for a table or chair. Two decorated pumpkin-shaped stones divided vertically through the middle so that the flat part abuts the wall were found — one, *in situ*, at the southwest corner of the structure, and another in the debris nearby. When placed on the stone base on the northwestern back end of the structure, the latter fitted so well that there could be no doubt of its original location. The straight, back sides of these two decorated, rounded stones each have a vertical recess carved into them corresponding with a square hole in the flat surface of the ashlars on which they were placed. These holes and slots probably served to hold up pillars or poles inserted into them. At the front end of the structure — the southeastern corner — is a large stone set deep in the ground, with only its carved rounded part protruding above the level of the flagstone pave-

199. The President of Israel, Prof. E. Katzir, and Prof. A. Gottschalk, President of the Hebrew Union College, inspecting the canopied structure

ment. The flattened top of this rounded stone has a shallow, circular recess carved into it. We conjectured that there probably was a similar carved stone at the opposite — northeastern — side of the structure where there is now an empty spot of plain earth.

These carved, decorated bases may have served to hold four columns or poles — two square ones in the rear and two round ones in the front — which probably supported a canopy. Similar canopied structures appear on contemporary Assyrian reliefs and on the bronze gates of Balawat, the summer palace of Shalmeneser III (858–820 B.C.E.). What purpose the canopied structure served at Dan we could not determine. Perhaps this was where the king or judge sat when he came to dispense justice at the gate: "Then the king arose, and sat in the gate. And they told unto all the people, saying, Behold, the king doth sit in the gate. And all the people came before the king" (2 Samuel 19:8). Or, it may have housed a statue of a deity, as is known from the cities of the Assyrian and neo-Hittite empires, in which case it was perhaps one of the high places located at the gate. Josiah's actions come to mind: "...and brake down the high places of the gates that were in the entering in of the gate of Joshua the governor of the city..." (2 Kings 23:8).

When we uncovered this structure and bench we were puzzled by their location in an exposed, undefended area outside the main gate. Why should public functions be conducted outside the city? We then noted that the stone pavement extended eastward, and when we continued the excavation the following year we had the answer. Some 8 m. further east, another threshold, 3.8 m. wide, was discovered consisting of a doorstop flanked by two large basalt slabs with holes for the doorposts. We had reached the outer gate that guarded the entrance to the paved square. It now became clear how the king and the elders "sitting in the gate" could conduct their business secure in the protection of an outer gate and guards. To the left, the outer gate itself was defended by a tower 5 x 3 m. in area, of which only the basalt foundations were found. On the right side of the entrance an ashlar construction and bench attached to the city wall were uncovered. The Israelite city wall continues in an easterly direction along the slope of the rampart with the flagstone pavement extending from it. That it was in use for a relatively long time is indicated by the repair and resurfacing at the eastern and southern end of the pavement.

The gate complex appears to have been quite elaborate. The proto-Aeolic capitals found in the 1992 season among the debris on the flagstone pavement may well have adorned the gate entrance. Chariots would have to be parked on the pavement since the steep incline made their ascent into the city difficult, if not impossible. What activities, we wondered, took

200.   The flagstone pavement south of the city wall and the city-gateway

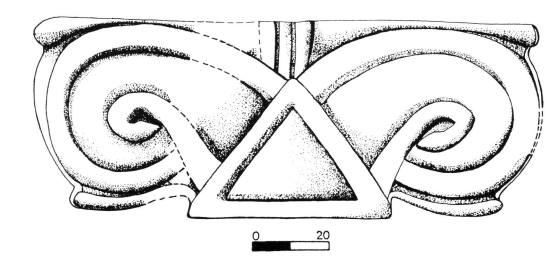

0   20

201.   Proto-Aeolic capital found on the flagstone pavement

place in the area — especially in the paved square between the outer and the main inner gates? We have already mentioned the stone structure at the main gate. Another tantalizing discovery, in 1971, of a step in front of the outer gate and of a well-dressed stone about 60 cm. high, caused considerable excitement. When the upper part of the stone first appeared we thought we had found a four-horned altar. We excavated the stone and its surroundings with great anticipation, wondering if it would bear an inscription and whether it was *in situ*. Why was it placed in front of the gate? Was there any significance to the somewhat elevated threshold? To all these questions there were no satisfactory answers. We thought that perhaps such a monolith in front of the gate might be similar to the ones identified as *mazzeboth* — standing stones at gate entrances. That this is indeed a possibility may now be considered in view of the results of the 1992 excavation season.

In the course of conservation and restoration work carried out by the Israel Antiquities Authority the northeastern section of the flagstone pavement between the gates was excavated. Some remarkable discoveries were made under the accumulated debris of the violent destruction covering the pavement. First, among the stone collapse, we uncovered an architectural element — perhaps a decorative capital unique in the annals of archaeology

202.   Unusual capital found in the destruction level of the gate (lying on its side)

203.   Five standing stones (*mazzeboth*?) to the right of the outer gate; en face

204.   Five standing stones (*mazzeboth*?) to the right of the outer gate; side view

in this country. Then, an even more remarkable find came to light: five undressed stones of heights and widths varying between 30 cm. and 50 cm., were set upright at the foot of the city wall. In front of these stones is a 30 cm.-high bench or table built of stone, 90 cm. wide and 2.2 m. long. At its eastern end is a wall 1.5 m. long and 50 cm. high. On the western end of the bench is a dressed stone 1.5 m. long. All these elements appear to have been built as one entity. The suggestion that the five stones are *mazzeboth*, "erected stones" often mentioned in the Bible was inescapable. The bench or table in front of them enclosed by construction on both sides, further suggested that they might be cultic in character. This was confirmed by the discovery, immediately to the west, of a relatively large assemblage of pottery vessels, some of them whole, in the same destruction level that buried the standing stone installation. They included incense bowls, plates, oil-lamps, and bowls. If we are right that the standing stones represent a cultic place, then the pottery vessels are part of offerings.

Thus the possibility that the paved area, in addition to its other functions, also served as a cult center assumes more credibility. The meticulous way in which the flagstone pavement was laid, the layout of the inner and outer gates, the unique decorated bases for the columns supporting the canopy, the buttressed outer walls of the gate chambers — all represent careful and well thought-out planning. Could we identify the historical figure capable of undertaking such an elaborate project? Could the date of its construction be determined?

When discovered, the gate complex was in ruins. The red mud-bricks on the piers of the gate and the thick layer of ash and destruction debris which covered the complex all testified to a violent end. A layer of debris 1 m. thick had to be cleared from the guard room before the floor was exposed. Such a "good" destruction level is a godsend to the archaeologist, for it enables him to date the last use of the building — notwithstanding

205. Vessels found next to the *mazzeboth*

his feelings for the people who suffered the calamity. In this area we were fortunate in finding not only sherds on the floor but also almost complete vessels. These included cooking pots, bowls, a jug, and storage jars. These vessels, dated to the 8th century B.C.E., are similar to the assemblage uncovered in subsequent seasons in a thick layer of destruction in Area T at the northern section of the site and dated to the second half of the 8th century B.C.E. Based on the ceramic evidence we concluded that the destruction of the gate complex took place in the second half of the 8th century B.C.E. and ascribed it to the Assyrian conquest of northern Israel by Tiglath Pileser III in 732 B.C.E. It is true that Dan is not mentioned in the annals of Tiglath Pileser or in 2 Kings 15:29 along with other cities that were destroyed, such as Ijon, Abel-beth-maachah and Hazor. These, however, were cities on the direct marching route of the invading army and hence were singled out for special mention. The other conquered cities, such as Dan, would have been covered by the more general "all the land of Naphtali," some of whose people were carried off as captives to Assyria by Tiglath Pileser III.

Just as the date of destruction was determined by pottery found on the floor of the gate, the date of the construction was indicated by pottery found under it. Beneath the gate we found an assortment of broken vessels spanning a long period — from the 3rd to the 1st millennium B.C.E. The latest sherds relevant for dating the gate included bowls, juglets, cooking pots, and jars from the first half of the 9th century B.C.E. Accordingly, the gate complex and city wall were built around 860–850 B.C.E. and remained in place until 732 B.C.E. Who then is to be credited with the construction of these magnificent structures? The historical sources for this period are meager. The northern kingdom of Israel was subject to internal instability, and only with the accession of Omri to the throne around 875 B.C.E. was a dynasty established that ruled for three generations — a relatively long period of time given the political upheavals in ancient Israel. Omri and his son Ahab put an end to the dispute with Judah in the south and established a strong relationship with Phoenicia to the west. Ahab's marriage to Jezebel, daughter of Eshbaal, king of Tyre and of the Sidonians (1 Kings 16:31), strengthened the alliance. During the reign of Ahab, the kingdom of Israel achieved considerable power, enabling it to defeat the Aramean army and causing Ben-hadad to say to Ahab "the cities which my father took from thy father I will restore, and thou shalt make streets for thee in Damascus" (1 Kings 20:34). It was a period of economic growth and expansion in Israel as well as in Judah.

Scholars credit Ahab with great construction projects which archaeological excavations have revealed in such ancient cities as Hazor and Megiddo.

Especially remarkable were the sophisticated water systems. The Bible disapproves of Ahab and his ways, but it was Ahab who led an alliance against Assyria in 853 B.C.E. with a large contingent of chariots and infantry. Ahab would obviously have been concerned about the security of his northernmost outpost. Whether for defence against Assyria or Damascus, Ahab is the most likely candidate for the building of the city walls and gate at Dan in the 9th century B.C.E. Moreover, he probably built the tower we found on top of the mound at the upper part of the flagstone pavement. The walls of this tower are constructed of large basalt boulders and the floor is covered with thick plaster on which a 9th century B.C.E. vessel was found.

The 9th century B.C.E. fortifications were not the first Iron Age defenses to have been built at the foot of the outer ramparts. Under the piers of the gate and the flagstone pavement, earlier structures were uncovered. The flagstone pavement was found on a 1 m.-thick layer of earth which in turn covers a massive stone construction. The wall between the two southern guard rooms was built partially over the corner of a building constructed of large basalt boulders which has been preserved to a height of 2.15 m. Traces of whitish plaster remained on the southern side of this building. The wall between the northern guardrooms also made use of the earlier building as a foundation. We followed the southern side of the structure to a distance of about 5 m. and could make out plaster which coated the building down to 3 m. below the level of the gate — without reaching the base level of the building. To this earlier phase of construction belongs a section of a stone pavement under the present floor of the gate. The existence of the 9th century B.C.E. gate precluded the extension of the excavation in this area.

Dated to the 10th century B.C.E., the construction of the earlier defenses was most likely undertaken by Jeroboam I, the son of Nebat, who set up the golden calf at Dan and made the city one of the religious centers of the northern kingdom. We know from the Bible that Jeroboam I was a capable builder, for he had previously fortified Shechem and Penuel (1 Kings 12:25). It may be that the fortifying of Dan was begun even before Jeroboam I and Ahab. The memory of the destruction of Stratum V of Dan in the mid–11th century B.C.E. must still have been fresh during the following two generations. The tribe of Dan, as the Canaanites of Laish before them, had depended on the earthen ramparts for protection, but the impregnability of these defenses had proven illusory. David and Solomon, both great empire builders, would not have ignored the defense of their northern outpost. Remains of large structures beneath the 9th century tower on the ridge of the mound are dated to the 11th–10th centuries

206. Reconstruction of the Israelite city-gates and wall: 1 — the paved piazza;
      2 — the outer gate; 3 — the main gate; 4 — the paved way; 5 — the upper gate

206a. Reconstruction of Israelite city-gate complex with flagstone pavement

B.C.E. They may indeed represent the beginning of a new defensive system which culminated a few decades later in the fortifications at the bottom of the earthen ramparts built by Ahab in the 9th century B.C.E. These, in turn, were strengthened in the 8th century B.C.E.

That Dan did not escape the vicissitudes that befell the northern kingdom during its relatively brief history is attested, for example, in 1 Kings 15:20: "So Ben-hadad...smote Ijon, and Dan, and Abel-beth-maachah, and all Cinneroth, with all the land of Naphtali." Later, however, the reign of Jeroboam II was a period of prosperity. The prophets Amos and Hosea minced no words in castigating the king and the upper classes for their accumulated wealth and the prevailing social injustice. As we have seen, the sanctuary was enlarged at that time, and the economic affluence of the kingdom enabled Jeroboam II to allocate resources also for strengthening the defenses of Dan. It was he, we believe, who built the upper gate in the second quarter of the 8th century B.C.E.

By the first half of the 8th century B.C.E. the lower gate and pavement had already been in existence for almost a hundred years. The flagstone pavement, 7 m. wide where it turns north, runs between stone walls, each about 90 cm. wide. The wall along the western side of the pavement continues northward for some 20 m. Besides serving the incoming and outgoing traffic, this impressive pavement was undoubtedly also used as a royal

207. The flagstone pavement leading to the top of the slope from the door-sill of
the main gate (below center)

processional and ceremonial way. But extensive changes were made in the
8th century B.C.E.: About 12 m. below the ridge, on the upward slope of
the flagstone pavement, we unexpectedly came upon an east-west wall,
1.2 m. wide and about 12 m. long, built across the pavement. This wall
impeded direct ascent to the city by forcing a would-be attacker to go
around it. At that point a new outer gate was built, with a 4 m.-wide
threshold and a doorstop in its center. North of the threshold are the
remains of a tower and a bench, and a layer of flat stones was placed on
top of the previous pavement to raise the floor level. This raised flagstone
pavement served as a large 20 x 10 m. piazza. At its western end is a rectangular hall measuring 5 x 2 m., with a bench along its walls, and on its left,
a stepped structure somewhat similar to the one at the main gate below.
Additional layers of flagstones provided easier access to the entrance of the
upper gate. The upper gate construction made use of the original massive
stone core of the Middle Bronze Age Canaanite rampart, and perhaps also
parts of an earlier gate of that period. To strengthen the gate structure, the
builders also incorporated some previously existing defensive elements of
the Israelite period.

The upper gate is of the four-chamber type, straddling the paved road
which is 4 m. wide here. The northern chambers measure 4.6 x 3.3 m.

208.   The eastern chambers of the upper gate (Stratum II)

209. Proto-Aeolic capital found in secondary use in a wall of the upper gate structure
      (Stratum II)

each. The floors, made of stone, are about 10 cm. higher than the roadway. The stone-built walls of the chambers are 1.2 m. thick and are preserved to a height of 1.3 m. Stones including ashlars of earlier buildings were used in the construction. Among them is half of a capital with a palmette carved in relief — an architectural element in the proto-Aeolic or proto-Greek style — of the type found at royal Israelite cities such as Jerusalem, Megiddo and Hazor. It must have come from an earlier monumental building, perhaps a palace or a temple somewhere in the city. The masses of mud-brick found all over the flagstone pavement made it abundantly clear that this was the material of which the superstructure of the upper gate was built. Here was found a seal with an engraved representation of a chariot and three soldiers.

The upper gate and the change in the direction of the approach to the city were designed to ensure additional security, for by the 8th century B.C.E. the city wall at the foot of the slope and the gate itself were no longer considered sufficient protection. The place originally chosen for entering the city had been determined by convenience: In earlier days, a Middle Bronze Age gate existed on the southern flank of the earthen ramparts and this location was deemed suitable for entry also in the Israelite period. This was, no doubt, one of the reasons why Jeroboam I and Ahab built the fortifications where they did. In the days of Jeroboam II however, this convenient location must have been considered detrimental to the defensive system, and an indirect approach to the city was effected by erecting a wall across the pavement, forcing a detour midway to the ridge, and then building an outer gate with a tower, a flagstone piazza, and an upper gate at the top — a complex strikingly similar to the one at the foot of the city ramparts.

This upper gate complex did not prevent Dan from falling to the Assyrians. Apparently the city was not completely destroyed, but its defenses surely were. The Assyrian conquerors could not allow the elaborate defenses of Dan to remain operational. Dan became an open, undefended city. The flagstone pavement continued to serve the inhabitants and the worshipers at the sanctuary who flocked to the city — the major civilian and religious center in the north of Israel.

How impressive and formidable the Israelite defenses were can now be seen following the restoration work carried out by the Antiquities Authority on behalf of the Israel Government Tourist Corporation. Excavation of the city wall was extended 12 m. to the west and uncovered a new buttress or bastion. The city wall has been raised 8 m. above bedrock in order to reach the height of the ascending paved road. The exterior southern and eastern walls of the outer gate were both found to have a slight offset in the middle. The eastern wall ends in the projecting tower of the outer gate. The ashlar doorjambs of the outer gate have been restored to at least 1.5 m. above the threshold and the sloping pavement of the outer courtyard. Approximately 75 sq. m. of this courtyard were known from previous seasons; today 375 sq. m. have been exposed, and the pavement may indeed extend further east. This pavement shows many signs of repairs. It slopes steeply in several directions and concave depressions suggest the presence of walls and rooms, or open spaces below, but they may also hint at the possibility of damage by earthquake. The discovery in the destruction level of large limestone blocks and remains of three proto-Aeolic capitals testifies to the elaborate construction of the Israelite gate.

0 ━━━━━━━━━━━━ 1

210.   Seal with depiction of a chariot and charioteers found in the area of the upper gate

CHAPTER XII — THE CITY FROM THE 8TH CENTURY B.C.E. AND AFTER

A meticulously-laid flagstone pavement was uncovered in the center of the city (Area M). About 130 sq. m. have been exposed so far, but it appears to extend in all directions. This large paved area between the upper gate to the south and the sanctuary to the north apparently served as a public meeting ground. A similar pavement was found southeast of the sanctuary. The ceramic evidence dates these pavements to the middle of the 8th century B.C.E., and they may be attributed to Jeroboam II who built the upper gateway and made important additions to the sanctuary. During his reign, which corresponds to Stratum II, building activity extended all over the city. We uncovered remains of large public buildings and smaller dwellings of the 8th century B.C.E. in every excavated area. The expansion and development of Dan as a result of the prosperity following Jeroboam II's successful wars is evidenced also in the rich repertoire of finds, which include the head of a faience figurine (in Area Y) and an unusual cup-and-saucer vessel with traces of soot (in Area K). This vessel was used as an oil-lamp — perhaps in a cultic context. In the 1988 excavation season we discovered an amphora handle stamped with the name "Zecharyo" in ancient Hebrew script, dated epigraphically to the middle of the 8th century B.C.E. The name consists of the verb "remember" and the theophoric ending *yo*. A king by this name (Zachariah, in the King James version) is mentioned in 2 Kings 14:29. He was the son of Jeroboam II and ruled the northern kingdom for six months before he was assassinated. It is probably pure coincidence that the name of the owner of the vessel is also the name of a contemporary king, but perhaps this amphora did after all come from the royal stores.

A room containing over 300 juglets that was uncovered on the southern slope of the mound also belongs to this period. From their large number and their position these juglets probably had been set on shelves, perhaps in a shop, to be purchased by the people as they came up through the gates to the city from the villages in the plain below. Among the finds is a sherd with a Hebrew inscription "[belonging] to Amoz [or Amaziah]." The name is not uncommon in the Bible, the most famous example being the name of the prophet Isaiah's father (Isaiah 1:1).

211.   Faience figurine from Area Y

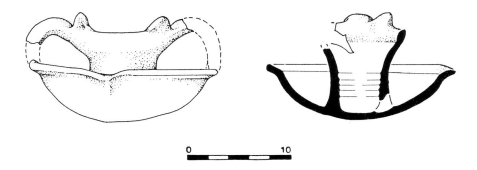

212.   Cup-and-saucer vessel (used as an oil-lamp?) from Area K (Stratum II)

0   1

213. Stamped seal impression of "Zecharyo"

214.   Part of a hoard of 8th century B.C.E. juglets (Stratum II)

215.   Inscription of Amoz, 8th century B.C.E.

Stratum II of Dan came to an end at the time of the Assyrian conquest
of northern Israel by Tiglath Pileser III in 733–732 B.C.E. Large assemblages of entire vessels were discovered in this stratum. Most of the types
represent developments of 9th century B.C.E. pottery, although they also
have new characteristics. In the amphoras, for example, the necks are
shorter and the shoulders more rounded. The large bowls still have
carinated rims, but the wealth of slips and burnishing typical of 9th century
B.C.E. pottery now dwindles. New types appear for the first time —
decanters and amphoras with carinated shoulders, elongated bodies and
pointed bases — which will be characteristic of the succeeding stratum.

What happened to the population in the wake of the Assyrian attack is
not clear. From the Assyrian annals, and from a brief reference in the Bible
(2 Kings 17:6,24), we learn that the indigenous population of the country
was taken captive and exiled, and other peoples brought in their place.
How many were exiled and how many were brought in their place we are
not told. The Israelite population was too large to have been transferred
en masse. The appeal of King Hezekiah of Judah to the remnants of the
northern kingdom (2 Chronicles 30:5–11) to join in his religious reforms
attests to the existence of a kindred population at that time. The passage
specifically mentions the tribes of Ephraim and Manasseh and the Galilean
tribes of Zebulun and Asher. The mother of Amon the king of Judah and

the mother of King Jehoiakim came from Galilee in the 7th century B.C.E. (2 Kings 21:19; 23:36). Groups of Israelites doubtless remained in Galilee in places the Assyrians had not repopulated. This may well account for their large number in later times, for example, in the Hasmonean period.

The Land of Naphtali, including perhaps also Dan, became part of the Assyrian province of Megiddo. The destruction of the Israelite gates at Dan did not spell the abandonment of the city. The archaeological evidence shows that following the Assyrian conquest Dan revived rapidly, no doubt thanks to its favorable location and the importance of its sanctuary. A new phase in the occupational history of Dan begins with Stratum I. The city now replaced Hazor as the main center of population in the Hulah Valley, a position it maintained until the Babylonian conquest. Indeed, in the 7th century B.C.E. Dan enjoyed its greatest period of expansion since the Early Bronze Age in the 3rd millennium B.C.E. All available space was utilized. The houses now reached the very top of the ridge around the site. Well built stone walls of houses are found everywhere and the public buildings are 15–20 m. long. Streets, some of them paved, attest to proper town planning. During the period of Stratum I the affinity to the Phoenician and coastal cities becomes more pronounced. An Assyrian-type vessel and part of a Corinthian juglet were also found in this level. In Area M houses were built on the layer of debris. Large, varied assemblages of pottery of different forms and types were found in the houses and courtyards of this stratum. Some of the types, such as the decanters and the amphoras with carinated shoulders and elongated bodies, continue the traditions of the previous stratum. For the first time, there now appear large, heavy bowls known as *mortaria*, and types deriving from Assyrian ceramics such as bottles and carinated bowls. The finds of this period include storage jars, decanters, jugs, cooking pots, *mortaria* and bowls dated to the middle of the 7th century B.C.E. Among the vessels are types found in Phoenicia and the Mediterranean coast of the country and in the East — perhaps indicative of Dan at this time having been a center of trade with strong ties throughout these regions. Of special interest was the discovery of an amphoriskos strikingly similar to one found in the tomb of Adoninur at Amman in Transjordan. The burial cave was excavated in the 1940s and among the finds was a seal bearing the inscription translated as: "To Adoninur the servant of King Aminadav." Aminadav is known from the Assyrian sources as the king of Amon, who paid tribute to Assurbanipal (668–635 B.C.E.). The amphoriskoi from Amman and Dan may thus be dated to the mid–7th century B.C.E. Possibly, trade contacts between the Mediterranean coast and Transjordan were conducted by way of Dan, bringing a new population element into the city.

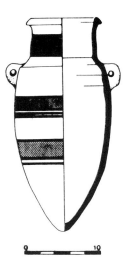

216.   Decorated amphoriskos similar to one from the tomb of Adoninur at Amman
       (see also Pl. 42)

Of considerable significance was the discovery in 1968 of a Phoenician
inscription in Area H, on the southern side of the mound. On the shoulder
of an amphora were the letters *l b ʿ l p l t* in Phoenician script, read as: "To
Baal Pelet" — "[belonging] to [a person by the name of] Baal Pelet," meaning "may Baal save or redeem." This name is reminiscent of the names
Elishama, Beeliada, and Eliphalet (1 Chronicles 14:7). We do not know
this individual's identity, but the name may appear on another amphora
fragment bearing the two letters *lamed* and *tet*, found twenty years later in
a 7th century B.C.E. level in Area T, near the spring. These two letters
may be the last two of the name *bʿlplt* (Baal Pelet), and if so, would be the
same as that on the amphora found in 1968. Perhaps both amphoras
belonged to the same person. The inscribed sherd was found with other
vessels in the 1988 excavation season in the western section of the sacred
precinct, which in that period apparently served as a residential quarter.
Perhaps these were the remains of the dwellings or houses of functionaries
officiating in the religious rites at the sanctuary. Here, clearly-defined
phases of new construction could be distinguished. The pilaster wall of the
large public building now served as the northern wall of the new houses,
while the remaining walls were newly built in the 7th century B.C.E.
Some of the rooms have stone floors while others have floors of gravel and
beaten earth. The sills between the rooms were found intact. The vessels
include a 7th century B.C.E. Cypro-Phoenician juglet, a bar-handle bowl,
several *mortaria*, and other pottery. Between the stones of one of the walls

217.   Seventh century B.C.E. house, and one of the rooms from Area H (Stratum I)

218. Phoenician inscription: "To Ba'al-Pelet" on shoulder of jar from Area H; potsherd with letters *lt*, Area T

219. Vessels dated to the end of the 7th–beginning 6th centuries B.C.E. from
      Area M (see Figs 220, 221)

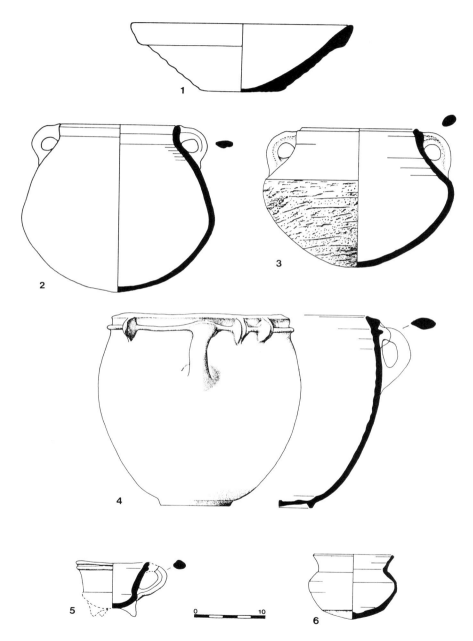

220.   Vessels of the 7th–6th century B.C.E.: 1 — *mortaria*; 2,3 — cooking pots; 4 — krater; 5 — cup; 6 — Assyrian-type bowl

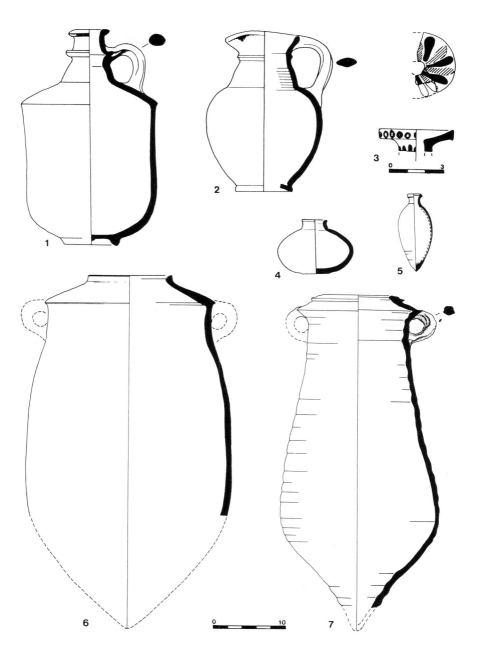

221. Additional vessels of the 7th–6th century B.C.E.: 1 — decanter; 2 — jug;
3 — Corinthian vessels; 4, 5 — Assyrian-type bottles; 6, 7 — amphoras

222. Remains of 7th century B.C.E. buildings; note tabun in lower photograph

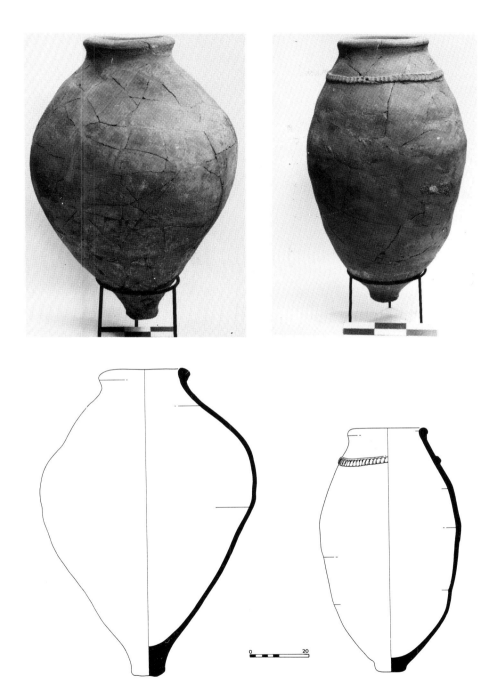

223. Two pithoi of the 7th century B.C.E. from Area T (see also Pl. 43)

224.   Seal with horned animal (ibex?)

we found a 7th century B.C.E. scaraboid seal incised with an animal, perhaps an ibex.

Although there is no evidence of destruction the next phase of Stratum
I represents a complete architectural change. A wall was built on top of the
pilaster wall, and in a room attached to this new wall two large, complete
pithoi were found. The domestic nature of these buildings is attested by
the discovery of three complete tabuns, or ovens, near the houses. Numerous decanters, amphoras, cooking pots, bowls, *mortaria* and oil-lamps represent the rich material culture of the 7th-beginning of the 6th century
B.C.E. The prosperity of the 7th century city is evident in each excavated
area. In Areas B and H, buildings — some of them quite massive with
1.2 m.-thick and 30 m.-long stone walls — were found at the edge of the
mound. The large city of Stratum I came to an end with the Babylonian
conquest of the country. Dan suffered the destructive impact of the Babylonian army on its march southward to Jerusalem (cf. Jeremiah 4:15; 8:16)
and may have been attacked earlier by the Egyptians when they came to
the assistance of Assyria in 616, and again in 609 B.C.E. The Egyptians

were defeated in Carchemish but they held sway over the country for a few years until Nebuchadnezzar, king of Babylon, gained possession of the entire region in 604 B.C.E. The Babylonians did not introduce many changes in the provincial organization they inherited from Assyria. During the sixty years of Babylonian hegemony, Dan seems to have been left to itself. Of this period were found remains of badly preserved walls.

With the conquest of Babylon in 539 B.C.E. by the Persians, Dan, along with the rest of the country, fell to King Cyrus of Persia. The country remained under Persian rule until the time of Alexander the Great. In the 200 years of Persian domination, Dan was probably incorporated into the Persian administrative district "Beyond the River," but Persian rule does not seem to have had any effect on Dan as an urban center. The Persian kings who passed through the country on their campaigns against Egypt used the coastal route and Dan probably lost much of its importance. However, we must be careful in making such statements, for although the excavations did not reveal any significant remains of the period, we must always bear in mind that the excavated areas represent only a fraction of the entire mound. Perhaps the Persian strata of occupation will be found under the Hellenistic remains east of the sanctuary.

During the Hellenistic period Dan recovered somewhat from its temporary decline. In a probe carried out east of Area T remains of buildings of this period came to light. The dense vegetation prevented further excavations there, and the nature of these remains could not be determined, but they seem to be buildings of monumental proportions. At the southern part of the mound, the archaeological evidence also reflects the changes made in the Hellenistic period. The entrance to the city and the approach to the sanctuary continued to be from the south. The rubble covering the monumental flagstone pavement was cleared, and close to the ridge, the pavement was raised and rebuilt partly on the debris of fallen mud-brick. The gateway between the chambers of the upper gate continued in use, but the chambers were blocked and no longer served as guard-rooms. At the bottom of the new walls enclosing the chambers, stone benches were built along the gateway, providing rest for the weary. A juglet found between the stones blocking the chambers dates this construction to the 3rd century B.C.E.

In the Roman period the settled areas of Dan were considerably reduced. Our excavations into the grid squares revealed no domestic remains of the Roman period, although some such occupational evidence was encountered while surveying the southern part of the mound — probably belonging to the village of Dan mentioned by Eusebius, a 4th century C.E. Byzantine bishop and historian from Caesarea. That it was primarily an

225. Statue of Aphrodite found in the fields near Tel Dan, copy of the Roman period

agricultural community could be seen from the water installations and terraces uncovered above the ruins of the Israelite occupational strata at the foot of the mound. Between the outer and main Israelite gates, a wall built across the pavement that had been in use for centuries, now prevented access into the city, and the flagstone pavement no longer served as a main thoroughfare. Halfway up the flagstone pavement, two tombs of the Roman period were discovered. East of these tombs a water cistern had been constructed, and a cistern with a mosaic floor was dug into the pavement in the main piazza between the Israelite city gates. Water was conveyed to the cistern through clay pipes, and a regulating pool controlled the flow of water — also to the cistern dug among the ruins of the northeastern tower of the Israelite gate. The entrance to the city and the approach to the sanctuary must be sought elsewhere.

Water installations seem to be the trademark of the Roman period at Dan, but beyond this we know very little about the people who resided here at the time. Eusebius mentions only that a village existed four miles from Paneas (Banias) on the road to Tyre, and it appears that soon after his time the site was abandoned. The only finds from later periods are a number of 13th–15th century C.E. tombs found when we began our rescue excavation. The stones of earlier occupation were used in the construction of the tombs, and some Islamic pottery and jewelry were found with the burials.

The name Dan, from the Hebrew verb "to judge" was kept alive in the Arabic name Tell el-Qadi meaning Mound of the Judge, while the Arabic names ʿEin el-Dan and Nahr el-Dan for the spring and the river preserve the tradition of the ancient name Dan. The Hebrew name was adopted in 1939 by Kibbutz Dan when it settled on the plain south of the mound.

226.   The Aramaic inscription from Tel Dan

POSTSCRIPT — THE ARAMAIC STELE FROM TEL DAN

The twenty-seven years of excavation at Tel Dan produced very little written material — until on 21 July 1993 an inscribed basalt stone was found. The stone — a broken fragment of a larger block — was found in secondary use in a wall bordering the eastern part of the large pavement, or piazza, in front of the outer Israelite city-gate. Although, as mentioned in Chapter XI above, we knew of this pavement for some time, it was completely excavated only in 1993 in connection with conservation and restoration work carried out by the Antiquities Authority and the Israel Government Tourist Corporation.

The almost square pavement covers an area of approximately 400 sq. m. At its east side is a wall that underwent considerable change, including damage caused by the construction of a water channel during the Roman

227. The stone-paved piazza in front of the outer Israelite gate; the city wall is in the background; the inscribed stone was found in the wall at the right; note also one of the hinge-pivots *in situ* in its hinge-socket

228.   The threshold of the newly-discovered gate at the southern end of the paved piazza with the basalt hinge-pivots *in situ* in their hinge-sockets

period. We could not determine whether the stone pavement extends further east. Because of later construction, the limits of the pavement are also not clear on the southern side, although there is sufficient evidence to suggest that it extended further south to the threshold of a previously unknown gate. At both ends of this threshold round, bowl-shaped door-hinge sockets are recessed in the stone. The unique feature of this gate is the discovery of two hemispherical basalt stone hinge-pivots having square holes in their flat tops into which the door posts were fitted. These hinge-pivots together with the entire door assembly turned in the sockets.

The inscription on the basalt slab fragment was first noted by the surveyor of our expedition, Gila Cook. Taking a closer look at the stone while it was still *in situ* in the rays of the afternoon sun, we could see the engraved lines and contours of letters quite clearly. The stone was easily removed, for only a small part of it was embedded in the ground. Turning the stone to face the sun, the letters stood out even more. The words separated by dots sprung to life. It appeared to be a fragment of a large monumental inscription.

The fragment measures about 32 cm. high by 22 cm. at its maximum width. From the nature of the break it appears that the original basalt block had been smashed in antiquity, and we estimated its original size to have been about 1 m. high and perhaps 55 cm. wide. According to Ariel Heimann of the Geological Survey of Israel who examined the mineral content of the stone, the material is local basalt. The face of the stone was smoothed for writing, as was one of its sides. The chisel used was probably of iron with rounded edges since none of the letters show sharp corners.

The latest possible dating for the secondary use of our fragment could be determined by the date of the destruction level covering it — the third quarter of the 8th century B.C.E., the time of Tiglat Pileser III's conquest of northern Israel in 733/32 B.C.E. The stele fragment was thus set into the wall sometime before that date; how much earlier is difficult to say. The relatively small amount of pottery collected from the level beneath the basalt fragment contained nothing later than the middle of the 9th century B.C.E. This suggests that the stele was broken up around that time, so that it would have been erected during the first half of the 9th century B.C.E.

When a level of destruction dated to that time was discovered in the sanctuary area, we ascribed it to Ben-Hadad's attack of Dan mentioned in 1 Kings 15:20. Sometime later the sanctuary was rebuilt, probably by Ahab. It was also Ahab who fortified the town with a massive city wall and complex gate system, perhaps following his victory over the Aramaeans at Aphek. Now that we have the fragment of this Aramaic stele, we wonder if it refers to these incidents.

Of the original inscription, thirteen lines have been at least partially preserved, with only three letters at the top, five at the bottom, and fourteen at the widest section. Line 5 is 22 cm. long. The language is Old Aramaic and the script may be dated to the 9th century B.C.E. on paleographic grounds. Since the letters in each line comprise only a small part of the text, any reconstruction must remain tentative. The translation of a preliminary reading might be:

1. (?)
2. ...my father...
3. ...and my father lay down (died) he went to...
4. rael formerly in the land...
5. I . Hadad went before me...
6. ...my king and I slew of (them...[cha?])
7. riots and two thousand horsemen...
8. the king of Israel and (?)...
9. ...House of David and I...
10. (?) land of Ham(?)
11. other...
12. (ru)led over Is(rael?)...
13. siege upon(?)...

0   10 cm.

Since the text is very fragmentary and no name of a king — either of Aram or Israel or Judah — has been preserved, the Dan stele fragment may conceivably be attributed to almost any king of Aram who, according to the extant sources, fought against Israel in the 9th century B.C.E. The mention of the "House of David" in Line 9 indicates that a king of Judah was involved in the events described in the stele. This is the first time that the royal name "David" or the expression "House of David" has been found outside the Bible.

The passages in 1 Kings 15:16–22 and 2 Chronicles 16:1–6 are the only accounts of the Israel-Aram war in Galilee, and it is therefore tempting to relate the Dan stele to it. Ben-Hadad I, bribed by Asa king of Judah, attacked Baasha king of Israel: "And Ben-Hadad hearkened to King Asa, and sent the commanders of his armies against the cities of Israel, and conquered Ijon, Dan, Abel-beth-maachah, and all Chinneroth, with all the land of Naphtali" (1 Kings 15:20). This campaign is dated to ca. 885 B.C.E. Could Ben-Hadad have erected the stele at Dan in commemoration of his victories?

The word "my king" in Line 6 seems to indicate that whoever composed the inscription was a dependent of the king. Since in the 9th century B.C.E. the kings of Aram-Damascus were sovereign, the stele may have been erected by one of the captains of the Damascene king, perhaps one of the "commanders" referred to in the above passage, who might have been appointed governor of Dan and its vicinity. However, as the inscription seems to emphasize the writer's right to the throne, and even mentions "my father's land," the writer himself may have been a royal personage.

All of this must remain in the realm of learned conjecture until additional evidence turns up. A joint paper by the present author and Joseph Naveh on this fragmentary text has been published in the *Israel Exploration Journal* 43 (1993).

Bibliography

Biblical quotes are from the Revised Standard Version.

Albright, W.F., "The Jordan Valley in the Bronze Age," *Annual of the American Schools of Oriental Research* VI (1926): 16 ff.
_____ , "Palestine in the Earliest Historical Period," *Journal of the Palestine Oriental Society* XV (1935): 193 ff.
Barnett, R.D., "Layard's Nimrud Bronzes and their Inscriptions," *Eretz Israel* 8 (1967), pp. 1 ff.
Biran, A., "A Mycenaean Charioteer Vase from Tel Dan," *Israel Exploration Journal* 20 (1970): 90 ff.
_____ , "Une tribune anarchique: Dan," *Bible et Terre Sainte* 125 (1970), pp. 4 ff.
_____ , "Tel Dan," *Biblical Archaeologist* 37 (1974): 26 ff.
_____ , "Tel Dan — Five Years Later," *Biblical Archaeologist* 43 (1980): 168 ff.
_____ , "Two Discoveries at Tel Tan," *Israel Exploration Journal* 30 (1980): 89 ff.
_____ , "The Discovery of the Middle Bronze Age Gate at Dan," *Biblical Archaeologist* 44 (1981): 139 ff.
_____ , "To the God who is in Dan," *Temples and High Places in Biblical Times* (Jerusalem, 1981), pp. 162 ff.
_____ , "The Triple-Arched Gate at Tel Dan," *Israel Exploration Journal* 34 (1984): 1 ff.
_____ , "Die Wiederentdeckung der alten Stadt Dan," *Antike Welt* 15 (1984): 27 ff.
_____ , "The Dancer from Dan, the Empty Tomb and the Altar Room," *Israel Exploration Journal* 36 (1986): 168 ff.
_____ , "Histoire de deux villes," *Archéologie, art et histoire de la Palestine"* (Paris, 1988), pp. 55 ff.
_____ , "The Collared-Rim Jars and the Settlement of the Tribe of Dan," *Annual of the American Schools of Oriental Research* 49 (1989): 71 ff.
_____ , "Tel Dan Scepter Head," *Biblical Archaeology Review* XV (1989): 29 ff.
_____ , *Dan. 25 Years of Excavation at Tel Dan* (Tel Aviv, 1992) (Hebrew); and see list of Hebrew reference works: p. 17.
Kaplan, J., "Further Aspects of the Middle Bronze Age II Fortifications in Palestine," *Zeitschrift des deutschen Palästinavereins* 91 (1975): 1 ff.
Malamat, A., "The Danite Migration and the Pan-Israelite Exodus Conquest: A Biblical Narrative Pattern," *Biblica* 51 (1970): 1 ff.
Mazar, A., *Archaeology of the Land of the Bible* (New York, 1990), *passim.*
Mazar, B., "The Philistines and the Rise of Tyre," *The Israel Academy of Sciences and Humanities Proceedings* 1/7, pp. 1 ff.
_____ , "The Middle Bronze Age in Canaan," *The Early Biblical Period* (Jerusalem, 1986), pp. 1 ff.
Paar, P.J., "Fortifications of Middle Bronze Age Palestine and Syria," *Zeitschrift des deutschen Palästinavereins* 84 (1968): 18 ff.
Robinson, E., *Biblical Researches in Palestine* Vol. III (London, 1841), p. 358.

Schulman, A.R., "An Enigmatic Egyptian Presence at Tel Dan," *Festschrift Jürgen von Beckerath, Hildesheimer Ägyptologische Beiträge* (1990), p. 235 ff.

Yellin, J. and Gunneweg, J., "Instrumental Neutron Activation Analysis and the Origin of Iron Age I Collared-Rim Jars and Pithoi from Tel Dan," *Annual of the American Schools of Oriental Research* 49 (1989): 133 ff.